Rome 26.XI.2004

To Chris,

Congratulations for your new
assignment with the hope
as interesting as your
photography was.

Sincerely

[GIANNI GIANSANTI]

VANISHING AFRICA

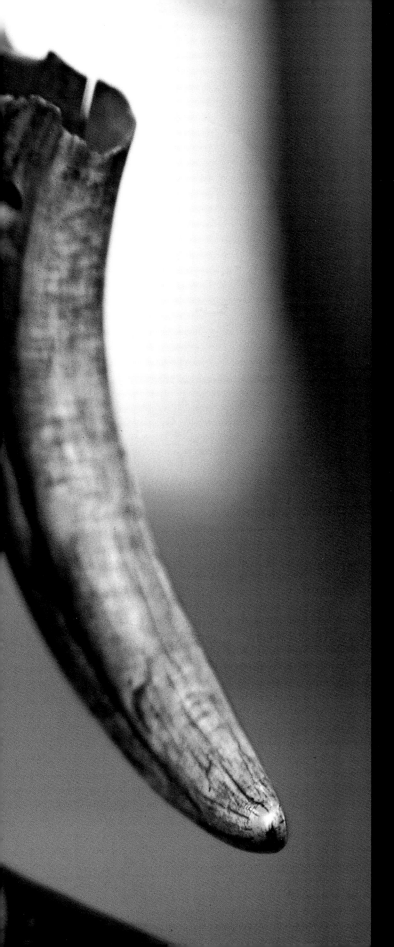

TEXT AND PHOTOGRAPHS
by GIANNI GIANSANTI

ETHNOGRAPHIC INTRODUCTIONS
by PAOLO NOVARESIO

PROJECT MANAGER AND EDITORIAL DIRECTOR
VALERIA MANFERTO DE FABIANIS

PROJECT AND GRAPHIC DESIGN
CLARA ZANOTTI

EDITORIAL COORDINATION
ALBERTO BERTOLAZZI
MARIA VALERIA URBANI GRECCHI

PHOTOGRAPHIC ASSISTANT
ADA MASELLA

WHITE STAR
PUBLISHERS

© 2004 White Star S.r.l.
Via Candido Sassone, 22/24
13100 Vercelli - Italy
www.whitestar.it
TRANSLATION: Richard Pierce

ISBN 88-544-0006-8

REPRINTS:
1 2 3 4 5 6 08 07 06 05 04

Printed in Italy - Color separation: Fotomec, Turin

CONTENTS

4

1 A Mursi warrior
displays his face
decorated with streaks
of plaster.

2-3 A Mursi girl wears
warthog horns on the
sides of her face.

5 The labret is a
characteristic feature of
Mursi and Surma
women.

TRAVEL DIARY

I N THE 17TH CENTURY, A PERIOD MARKED BY GREAT EXPLORATIONS, THE AFRICAN CONTINENT WAS CONSIDERED INACCESSIBLE, INHABITED BY WILD POPULATIONS AND FEROCIOUS ANIMALS, CHARACTERIZED BY UNKNOWN FAUNA AND FLORA, AND CONTROLLED BY MAGICAL FORCES.

The mysteries of Africa made the figure of the explorer even more fascinating: he faced great risks and danger in discovering lakes, rivers and mountains, thereby makng significant contributions to developing new maps and increasing our knowledge of the world.

Ethiopia was among Africa's most fascinating regions and was explored with particular interest and attention. Its history was rooted in dawn of humankind, and it was the land that yielded the remains of Lucy, who lived roughly three million years ago – the most ancient hominid known to science. In the early 19th century, the Italian Geographic Society commissioned Captain Vittorio Bottego to unveil the mystery of the Omo River's course. He organized an expedition of 250 askaris (native soldiers), equipped with donkeys and camels, and explored the river to its mouth, the point where its waters flowed directly into Lake Turkana, in southwest Ethiopia. With this discovery,

Bottego solved one of the enigmas of modern geography. During his return journey Bottego was killed by one of the native peoples who lived in large bands in that still remote and little known corner of Ethiopia. Even today, more than 50 ethnic groups populate this land; of the ten main groups, some live in areas still difficult to reach.

When White Star Publishers asked me to do a photo essay on the tribes that live in the lower Omo Valley, I was not immediately enthusiastic. Obviously, the project intrigued me, but it seemed to be a complicated undertaking. Furthermore, I had only vague ideas about Ethiopia. So I began to study the maps of the area and to gather information about its tribes, still far removed from any form of progress and civilization. The little information I got was summarized in a pair of guidebooks and in some chapters of rather old photo-story books.

I then grasped the importance of this project: in this age of instant communications in which I was able to reach the four corners of the world with a simple click on my mouse, there was in Ethiopia this area more or less the size of Switzerland yet remote in time and space beyond any stretch of the imagination.

I simply had to go there and take pictures. . . .

So we decided to organize a preliminary 'reconnaissance' in order to ascertain whether the idea

THE BANKS OF THE OMO

13 In the Bume area, luxuriant vegetation clothes the river basin.

was feasible. During that first journey I realized we would meet with many obstacle. The distances to be covered were long and fatiguing; the so-called roads were nothing more than barely visible dirt tracks. Even under normal conditions reaching some villages would be difficult and in the rainy season impossible: the tracks would be impassable and one would be blocked for days on end. Furthermore, to visit some tribes would require having armed rangers: every man in the Omo River Valley possesses a Kalashnikov – and no one hesitates to use it.

However, I was so fascinated by these people untouched by time that I decided to continue, aware that the later stages of the trips would be even more difficult: some villages were reachable only on foot or with a small plane. I realized that despite its many difficulties the project deserved to be undertaken.

It takes three days to reach the Omo Valley, but the journey is tantamount to making a leap of thousands of years back in time more than in space to understand what we were like before history changed humanity's course and destiny. This physical and mental journey would be necessary in order to see, get to know, and photograph a part of Africa that still existed but was rapidly disappearing.

If Africa leaves its mark on one, then Ethiopia leaves a huge gaping hole as wide as a dry riverbed.

I spent months with my maps preparing for one of the most complex journeys that could ever be planned. The problems were due in part to the difficulty in getting about in these areas, but mainly to lack of information: Colonel Mengistu's dictatorship has isolated Ethiopia from the rest of the world for over a decade. Lack of normal tourism and trade relations had slowed down the country's civil and economic development, but it had also helped to keep intact a fascinating region where it is possible to observe face to face a society still in its most archaic stage, uncontaminated by any type of consumerism.

We completed our expedition plan; it called for no fewer than fourteen outdoor camps in impenetrable zones. Then we were off. The day after our arrival at Adis Abeba, a Sunday morning, we left early, leaving a sleeping city behind us, the only exceptions being a few women who, wrapped in their veils, were headed to the churches to attend service. After about 62 rather monotonous miles, the scenery became more interesting: among umbrella acacia trees and volcanic hills we began to spot the first lakes that, in single file, accompanied us to our first layover at Arba Minch.

This first stage of the journey – about 280 miles – was the longest, and most of it was done on the Trans-African Highway up to the Shashemene junction, always traveling along the rise of the Rift Valley. We could not help thinking of this fascinating and incredible geological phenomenon that in a few million years will create a new sea right there where it now runs.

Situated at the crossroads between North and South, East and West, Shashemene is the unofficial capital of Ethiopia's Rastafarian community. With

15 left   A refreshing bath in the Neri torrent, next to the camp in the Mago National Park.

15 right An open-air shower in Tum Airport.

its shops flanked by brothels, music at full blast even in the streets, and coffee shops frequented almost exclusively by truck drivers, Shashemene is the last real sight before the great leap into the 'abyss.'

Toward evening we arrived at Arba Minch, 'the city of the 40 springs.' From our terrace at the Bekele Mola Hotel the panorama of the Abaya and Chamo lakes, separated by a hill called the Bridge of God, appeared to us in all its simple splendor. Then the last shower, the last phone call home, and the first mosquitoes, before the night's sleep erased all our worries about the journey that had just begun.

We spent the second night of camping out in a clearing in the Mago National Park listening to the roar of the Neri torrent and the aggressive shrieking of the numerous colobus monkeys. Upon awakening, we found the only the only way we could wash ourselves was to dive into the brown water that rushed by – certainly not very inviting, but at least it served the purpose. After breakfast we made plans for the day. Anyone who wanted to go to the Mursi villages had to be accompanied by armed rangers in order to avoid any unforeseen events or danger. In fact, our visit to the notorious Mursi people in Komba village was one of the most exciting stages of the trip. The Mursi warriors have a reputation of being excellent thieves, true professionals of this métier: according to legend, they can slip off their victim's shoes without his realizing it. I immediately thought of my cameras. We would have to keep our eyes open.

data:image/sketch;base64,...

FROM THE TRAVEL
JOURNAL "... I HAPPENED T
LOOK UP AND SEE MYSELF
SURROUNDED BY CURIOUS
CHILDREN WHOSE NAKED
BODIES BORE DIFFERENT
PAINTED PATTERNS."

17 The severe features of a
Mursi man become softer with
this rare smile.

We arrived at Komba after climbing up a rocky path and after an exhausting battle with the tsetse flies that reign supreme in the area. No sooner did the Mursi see us arrive than they surrounded us and began to touch us, asking for little gifts. Seeing them come upon us so suddenly disturbed us: rough, long-suffering faces attached to long, muscular and naked bodies. The odor of their skin was wild, almost animal. The women also arrived with labrets so large that they seemed to be mauling their half-open mouths.

We were enraptured, admiring them and observing their village, which consisted of no more than ten huts. We spent the whole day taking photographs of their faces, then we took photos of groups, the women and the children. In a fascinating but natural custom the villagers all had some ornament on their heads, an animal horn, iron rings, or wads of colored wool. In order to show their hospitality – and to get us to cough up a few *bir*, the local currency – they decided to have us witness part of the training for the Donga, the typical combat between the Mursi and the Surma. Inn the middle of the village two contenders began a mock fight, naturally being careful not to deal hard blows. I photographed this exhibition from a tree after after moving aside a large leafy branch that shadowed the entire arena. When the Donga practice ended, dances began as our visit wound down. It then took us three hours on the road to get back to our camp, but the fatigue was partly offset by the memory of this thrilling experience.

Our photo-journalism took us to other marvelous places and to people who were absolutely out of the ordinary. On one occasion we reached a Surma village on the Omo River's west bank. I was busy carefully packing my cameras in the courtyard of the military outpost of Tulgit when I happened to look up and see myself surrounded by curious children whose naked bodies bore different painted patterns.

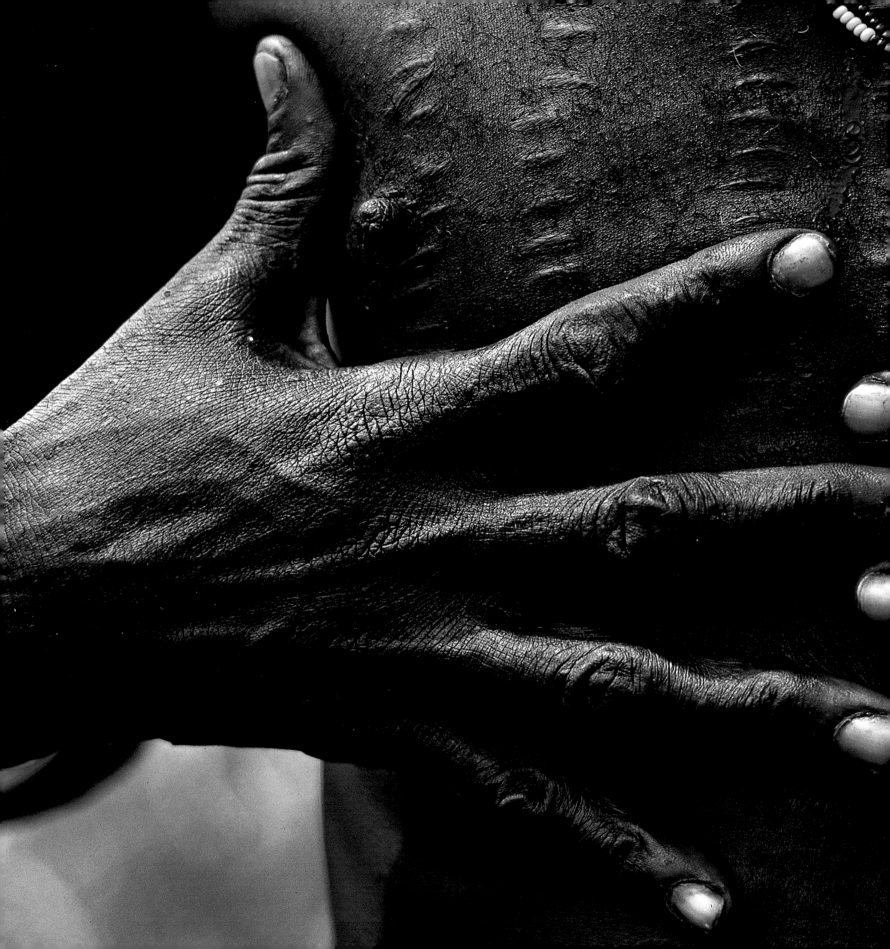

18-19 A Surma child whose face is painted yellow poses for the photographer.

20-21 A Mursi warrior proudly shows the scars on his chest.

22

ETHIOPIA 2003/04
"OMO VALLEY"

I was probably more surprised than they were, given the charm of their body painting and the elegance with which they was exhibited it. I took my cameras out of the bag in which I had just packed them and began to take photographs.

We left immediately after this experience. After driving along a long, dusty, uphill track we reached hill-top and the entire Omo River Valley appeared before our eyes, broad and infinite. Below we recognized Kibish: some sheet metal, a few huts, and three donkeys. Those poor creatures, with two soldiers, two porters and two helpers whom we recruited on the run during a stop at Mizan Teferi, accompanied us on our expedition to Kormu.

We set off at midday, an impossible time at that latitude, but we had a tough hike ahead of us. . . . We carefully chose the things needed for the trip, well aware that for six or seven days we would be living and working in precarious conditions: water, food, batteries and film had priority in this choice, as well as tents and medicine, of course.

During our personal Way-of-the-Cross journey we were forced to make many stops before arriving at Kormu. The asphyxiating heat sapped our energy and the hike facing us was a long and exhausting uphill haul. After walking for three and a half hours, we finally arrived at the foot of the hill where the village stood. The chief came to meet us and greeted us with the auspicious "Chally", which means "Everything's fine, is everything OK with you?" "Chally," we replied. "Except for the heat," I added. . . .

That night it rained cats and dogs. The following morning we found Fassil and Mekkonen, our helpers, wrapped in a sheet of plastic, while the soldiers and bearers had managed as best they could, perhaps in someone's hut. Fortunately there was a fire to warm our bodies and souls, while Fassil prepared a breakfast of eggs, milk and corn meal, which had been offered to us, together with a small goat, by Bar Gamoghy Doroty, the village chief, as a token of welcome.

In the meantime, the warm, intense dawn light was painting the field at the entrance to Kormu with red hues. A short distance away, Ghere Kara, the expert in body decoration, was beginning to paint the faces of some children, using empty Kalashnikov shells that had been dipped in damp dust smeared on a rock. The body painting continued later at the torrent, where the boys went to wash, while the girls were drawing water. Given the season, the torrent was dry, but they managed all the same, with the little water that came from a spring, to finish bathing. Circles, lines and geometric figures were the most common motifs of this

25 A woman painting the face of a child with a Kalashnikov shell.

body painting, which stayed intact on the skin until another attempt at washing wiped it off once more. Not one strip of skin was left unpainted: the face, chest, shoulders, legs and even the private parts were colored with this moistened dust, which was applied with the aid of Kalashnikov shells, small sticks and plant stalks, stems and crowns.

We returned to the village around noon. The heat was tremendous. We spent the afternoon taking photos here and there, and when evening arrived, we witnessed a fantastic spectacle: the full moon, in a clear sky studded with stars, illuminated the entire valley; all around were the lights of fires on the hills, indicating the presence of a hut, a family, a life.

During the course of our photo-story we witnessed unforgettable human experiences that gave rise to strong feelings. One of these was the flight on a Cessna plane that allowed us to photograph the entire course of the Omo River.

We had decided to set up base at Murle, in the Rift Valley Safaris camp: an out-of-the-way place in a stretch where the river meanders a lot, changing direction every 650 to 980 feet. This meant that we had a pickup truck come directly from the Adis Abeba with fuel drums so that we could refuel on

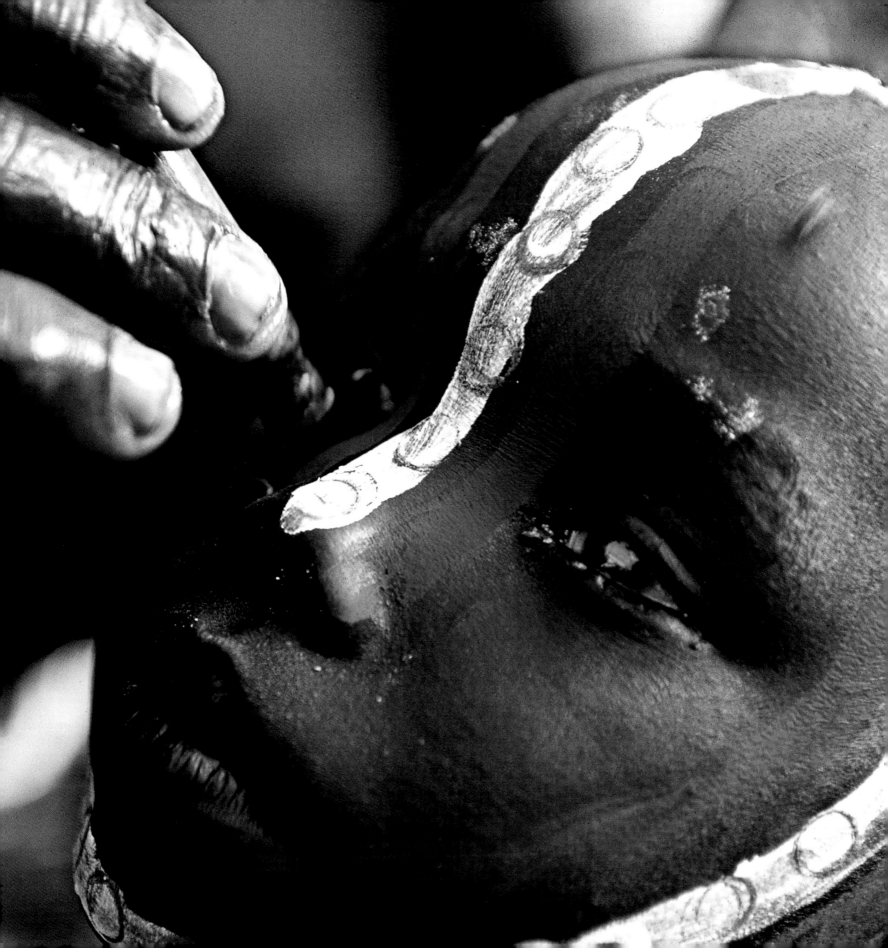

hel paese suae tempo!

FROM THE TRAVEL
JOURNAL
"... I WILL NEVER
FORGET THE VIEW OF
DAWN ILLUMINATING
THE FIRST VILLAGES
AND HUTS, WHICH
FROM ON HIGH SEEMED
TO BE DEFORMED BY
THE LONG SHADOWS."

our own on the spot during the three scheduled days of flights. Our plan called for fueling up at 6 a.m. and departure at 7 a.m., in order to take advantage of the best light conditions.

I will never forget the view of dawn illuminating the first villages and huts, which from on high seemed deformed by the long shadows.

Heading north in search of the Surma villages, we first passed over the Karo villages. At that point the river is less winding compared to its more southerly course. The Surma territory is hilly and the updrafts made our work difficult, as well as taxing the capacities of our pilot, Captain Salomon. We were airborne for a long time but took few pictures.

It was no easy task to go in search of villages at random, but it was the only possible solution: no map showed them. While flying over the Kibish Valley, we recognized Kormu, where we had spent several nights. Flying low over the huts was our way of saying goodbye to the villagers.

Viewed from above, the villages seemed to have 'urban' features that were not recognizable from the ground. The Dhaasanac, for example, have villages spread widely across dusty desert zones, while the Bume villages, although similar, are located in areas closer to the Omo River. The Karo, on the other hand, built their houses in orderly fashion next to the river, and the Surma lived in groups of huts in mountainous or hilly areas. The Mursi built their dwellings near the Mago River, while the Hamer had very extensive villages in which every family had its own hut and a large enclosure for the livestock.

After a day's work we suddenly decided to make a short stop at Turmi to buy a case of beer. Our base camp had none, and the idea of having beer, even warm beer, with our supper was tempting indeed. After twice flying low over the earthen runway – a method Captain Salomon used to drive away the cows and to spot the holes in the terrain – we landed

THE SHADOW ON THE DUST

The shadow of the Cessna looms over the Galeb village of Omorate, stirring the curiosity of the villagers.

Detail of a Mursi's eyes.

in a cloud of dust. All of a sudden about a hundred inhabitants came toward us while the motors were still running and the propeller was whirling dangerously. They had seen the plane fly over their heads and had come to have a look at us. Among the villagers were Gallo, Irish and Kala, who called us by name as soon as they recognized us and ran to hug us. After stopping at the Assafu bar, we took off while it was getting dark. We cast a final glance from above to admire the smiling faces of our friends: they were happy, and so were we. Twenty minutes later we would be landing at Murle, just in time, in this timeless land.

Kala, the young Hamer who welcomed us at Turmi, is part of one of our best memories of the expedition. Having come from a small village a half-hour's walk from Turmi, Kala, like all the adolescents in these parts, couldn't wait to leave puberty behind

him and finally become a 'man.' This was to happen on the most wonderful day of his life, when the jumping ritual was scheduled to take place. But Kala had another dream which was a carefully guarded secret that he revealed to me only on the last evening I spent at Turmi, when the fever that was afflicting him loosened his tongue. I saw Kala roll up the long garment that became a blanket in the evening, lie on the ground and prepare to sleep. From the opening in that improvised shelter that enveloped his head I caught a glimpse of his lucid, tired, bloodshot eyes.

"It's malaria," he whispered, "and it's the second time I've caught it in a short period." Then he collapsed, exhausted. I saw him sleeping in the light of the oil lamp while Anaylem was arranging the few things needed for supper in the hut that served as a kitchen. If Kala ever dreamed, I thought while giving him a quinine pill just before he dozed off, that night

The Jumping ritual, the Hamer 'jump on the bull.'

would be on the saddle of the bicycle he told me about. Tired of walking, he wanted a bicycle that would make it easier for him to get around, make him feel freer, and elicit his friends' admiration. . . . His work in the camp on Kaské River consisted of taking care of the few foreigners who ventured as far as Turmi: he helped them pitch their tents, kept guard over them, lent a hand in the kitchen, and climbed up the trees to gather mangoes.

When he awoke the next day, he felt much better, but he said no more about the bicycle. I thought that the malaria had probably played a nasty trick on him, inducing him to talk about things that he perhaps did not really think of or desire at all. We said goodbye, I gave him a T-shirt that he liked, paid him the amount of *bir* we had agreed upon, and hugged him. I didn't know if I would ever see him again. While our Toyota was moving off, Kala ran beside us and invited me to return to watch his jumping ceremony.

"Why not? Let me know," I shouted to him from the window while the car moved off in the dust.

A few days before writing the above I received a letter from Ethiopia. It was from Kala. I thought it would concern our leave-taking and would be a sort of invitation to the initiation ceremony. But to my surprise, after the usual polite queries about my health and my family, between the lines of that letter that bicycle reappeared, that impossible dream of a boy who was not yet a man – not the raving of a person with malaria fever, but a real dream.

I think the moment has come to grant his wish and make that young Hamer happy. It is also a way for me to feel a bit closer to that remote corner of Africa.

SIMPLE MOMENTS,
INSTANTS OF LIFE
THAT INSPIRE EVERY
WRITER TO CREATE A
POEM, JUST AS THEY
INSPIRE ME TO CREATE A
BEAUTIFUL 
IMAGE.

foco, per un breve tappa: quelli momenti di cruditá ci ... che depositiche per un attimo la te esprience di une giornale nunciate reoli.

ONCIATURA HAMMER

PROLE AR

Campo al chiarore di un fuoco

LA IO

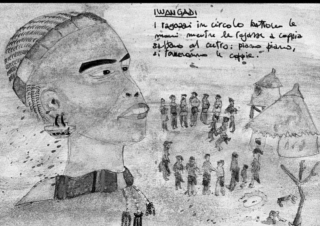

IWANGADI
I ragazzi in circolo battono le mani mentre le ragazze a coppia saltano al centro: piano piano, si formeranno le coppie.

Title page of the travel journal of Gianni Giansanti.

Weving the pictures with the Hamer in Turmi village.

In a dugout with the Karo in the murky waters of the Omo River.

Taking pictures of the Mursi from a precarious position near Komba.

Playing with a little girl in front of a hut.

A Karo woman grinding sorghum. The photographer in action.

34 and 35. An Erbore woman and a Surma warrior: the earrings, either spiral or round, are made of simple wrought iron.

A souvenir photo of a young Hamer girl before the Jumping ritual.

Putting the finishing touches to a portrait of a Surma warrior.

In the inn at the Djmeka market among drunk Hamer who are singing.

36-37 Horns and a labret are characteristic 'jewels' of the Mursi women, who look rather aggressive.

[PAOLO NOVARESIO]

THE RIVER OF MYSTERIES

F IFTEEN MILLION YEARS AGO A GIGAN- TIC RIFT THAT WAS AS MUCH AS 4.3 MILES DEEP AT SOME POINTS CUT THROUGH THE ROCKY SHIELD THAT CONSTITUTED THE TABLELAND OF EAST AFRICA, THUS GIVING RISE TO THE RIFT VALLEY.

The formation of this huge fissure, which traverses Africa from the Red Sea to Mozambique, was accompanied by massive eruptions. The consequences of this colossal geological cataclysm can best be seen in Ethiopia. On either side of the valley, which is dotted with lakes, there is a rugged highland, a tangle of mountains covered with a thick layer of black lava. It was here in this primeval landscape that the Omo River burrowed its way, cutting through the rock with patient erosive activity that lasted millions of years. The Omo rises on the slopes of Mount Amhara, about 62 miles west of the city of Adis Abeba. For most of its course the river flows between tall rock faces and consists of violent rapids. After the Gibé Bridge on the road linking Adis Abeba and Jimma, the Omo River penetrates wild, barren land where the roads are often mere cattle tracks that during the rainy season become trenches of mud and cannot be negoti-

ated by even the most robust vehicles. Two large reserves, the South Omo Park and the Mago National Park, have kept this strip of Africa intact. As they are extremely remote and almost totally lacking in the most elementary infrastructures, the parks in southern Ethiopia attract only a few dozen visitors per year, and plans for the development of tourism in this zone clash with a delicate and difficult political and ecological situation. Poaching for meat and ivory is a constant threat here. The rhinoceroses have disappeared, and the number of elephants, which are hunted mercilessly, is decreasing to an alarming degree. For hundreds of miles, as far as Lake Turkana, the banks of the Omo are virtually inaccessible. Since the river valley is infested by crocodiles and hippopotami, bordered by a thick rain forest and cursed with unhealthy climate, it has never been a communication and commercial route for the locals, but rather a barrier or obstacle to be surmounted or avoided.

Leaving the mountains behind and having absorbed its last affluents, the Omo flows gently into the arid trench of the Turkana.

The countryside changes drastically near the mouth of the river; the long-stemmed vegetation gives

ETHIOPIA

Adis Abeba

K'ok'a Lake

Ziway Lake

Omo River

Jima

Abyata Lake

Langana Lake

Shala Lake

R I F T   V A L L E Y

Awasa Lake

Omo River

Abaya Lake

SURMA   *Tum*

Tulgit

Chamo Lake

Kibish   *Kormu*

MURSI

Mago National Park

BANNA

BUME

KARO   **ERBORE**

KONSO

SUDAN

Labouk

HAMER

BORANA

Omo River

GALEB

El Sod

Turkana Lake

KENYA

PHOTO WORLDSAT INTERNATIONAL

way to prickly scrub interrupted here and there by sun-parched prairies. Only the profiles of the termite mounds, which sometimes reach a height of 33 feet, interrupt the absolutely uniform landscape. The river proceeds silently in wide bends toward the large basin that extends among the spurs of the Rift Valley for over 155 miles. The delta penetrates the lake like the fingers of a hand for quite a stretch, advancing sinuously between the well-defined banks covered with marsh vegetation. This particular phenomenon is due to the fact that the water of the Omo, fresh and lighter than the water so rich in soda of Lake Turkana, remains on the surface for a long time, and the gradually reduced speed of the current facilitates the deposit of sediment, which accumulates and forms banks that are in a continuous state of metamorphosis. The level of Lake Turkana had dropped about 50 feet) in the last two decades. The cause of this drastic decrease is ascribed to the climatic changes and the reduced flow of the waters of the Omo, which are constantly being used for irrigation. At the same time, the elimination of the original vegetation and the use of new lands for agricultural activities in the upper basin have brought about a significant increase in erosion and hence a rise in the amount of sediment carried by the river. The combination of these factors has triggered the rapid growth of the delta area: the only humid zone in an extremely arid region, the Omo River delta is destined to become one of the most important oases of biodiversity in this region of Africa.

Southern Ethiopia, far from everything, immobile and timeless, appeared for the first time on maps of the continent only a little more than a century ago. This last, mysterious terra incognita of Africa revealed its uncontami-nated, amazingly beautiful nature to the first European explorers. But most importantly, those long forgotten lands had hidden a complex mosaic of populations that had been isolated for centuries and that to this day have preserved their customs and practices, which originated in prehistoric times. The Dhaasanac, Surma, Mursi, Karo, Nyangatom and Arbore are peoples who are related to one another and who have mixed because of mysterious migrations in the past; but at the same time each one is proud of its differences and its own identity. There are 45 ethnic groups that live in the lower Omo Valley, a maze of languages and cultures that elude any kind of rigid clas-sification. The so-called Omo stocks have a subsistence economy based on agriculture and pastoral activities, with the addition of hunting and the gathering of spon-taneous fruit. They are merciless warriors who pay no heed to suffering, whether it be their own or others', yet they are able to transform brute force into an art. Thus, in their hands the battle with martial arts-like poles becomes a display of agility and elegance, a dance on tip-toes. Their bodies, painted with lime and colored oxides, look like frescoes come to life. And even their firearms, which arrived in that isolated area as the backwash of too many forgotten wars, are worn like ornaments.

Farther west, amid endless expanses of yellow grass, there is the life of the Hamer and Banna pastoralist groups, marked by spectacular rituals. The men are adorned with ostrich feathers, while the women are painted in bright red ocher: the cult of beauty is an intangible yet indomitable cornerstone of their social life. Not far away, beyond the banks of another river, the Woito, the totems of the Konso keep watch over the tombs of the ancestors: wooden stelae with angular faces standing before the backdrop of hills skillfully cultivated with corn and sorghum. The geometry of these fields and the clean, orderly villages disappear as if by magic as midday approaches. Like an imaginary frontier, the parched banks of solitary Lake Chew Bahir marks out the western edge of the territory of the Borana nomadic people. These deserts, a jumble of hot rocks and sand, are the arena of the epic seasonal migrations of the Borana in search of pastures and water for their livestock, which is their only means of subsistence in this ruthless environment. At the end of the 19th century southern Ethiopia, situated between the Nile lowlands and the desolate savannas of Somalia, was totally unknown. All the major African rivers, from the Nile to the Congo, had been navigated and explored. Only the Omo jealously guarded its secrets. Lacking concrete data, the geographers of the time formulated the most bizarre theories. Might the Omo be one of the source branches of the Juba? Or, by means of the Sobat, was it a tributary of the Nile? A third hypothesis was that this river was an independent water network. But where those muddy waters that flowed from the distant hills to the north ended, remained a mystery.

In the late 1880s the French explorer Jules Borelli followed the upper course of the Omo up the northern latitude of 6° 50', where the river makes a sharp turn westward, to trace and plot the confine between the provinces of Kaffa and Gemu-Gofa. In his description, based mostly on information gathering during his voyage, Borelli claimed that the Omo River, after making another wide curve southward, flowed into a large basin in the interior, which the natives called Lake Shambara. A few years earlier, the Scottish explorer Joseph Thomson had set off from the coast on the Indian Ocean and managed to cross over the borders of the Masai territory, reaching the Lake Baringo area. The natives told him that much farther on to the north was another large lake, Samburu. Were Thomson's Samburu and Borelli's fabulous Shambara the same lake? And if so, was it there that the Omo ended? Or did the river flow out of the lake and then merge with the Nile?

In reality, nothing was certain here. While Borrelli wandered along the vague frontiers of Kaffa, another expedition was marching from Zanzibar toward the interior. On 6 March 1888, after a year of travel, the column led by Count Teleki von Szek and his lieutenant Ludwig von Honel was trudging desperately through the hills of lava detritus that border the Rift Valley in northern Kenya. Suddenly, from behind a mound of black gravel there appeared before the exhausted men a huge stretch of water: like a mirage, Lake Turkana filled the entire arc of the horizon, "its scintillating dark green surface extending as far as the eye could see." Teleki solemnly named the new discovery Rudolf, in honor of his Imperial Highness, the Crown Prince of Austria and Hungary.

But a nasty surprise was in store for the explorers, who were suffering from thirst and privation: the crystal-clear water had such a high soda content that it was undrinkable. After days of doubts and uncertainties, Teleki and von Honel heroically decided to continue their trek along the east bank. One month later the expedition arrived in the territory of the Dhaasanac (whom Teleki calls the Reshiat), where they could finally find some food. Lake Stefanie was a few days' walk from there: in his account, von Honel describes it as an infernal bog swarming with dying fish, crocodiles and hippopotami stuck in the shallows. Lake Stefanie, or Chew Bahir, which was already subsiding to a marked degree, is now an arid stretch of salty mud. Upon returning to their base at Lake Rudolf with the intention of proceeding toward the west coast of the lake, the explorers confronted an unexpected obstacle: a large river, the Nianam, blocked their way. No ford in the river was to be found, and Teleki reluctantly had to abandon his plans. Retracing his tracks, he and his men got to Mombasa in a few months.

The results of Teleki's feat were extremely important. Lakes Rudolf and Stefanie filled the gap on the maps, together with the names of hitherto unknown mountains, marshes, rivers and populations. During the brief reconnaissance along the Omo (or Nianam), von Honel managed to gather information concerning the people of this region: in his journal he speaks of the Hamer, Bashada and Bume, giving a detailed description of their customs, including the use of the labret (a disk inserted to extend the lower lip. The course of the Omo remained totally unknown, but the way had been paved for further exploration. In 1895 Arthur Henry Neumann, a professional elephant hunter, went up the river as far as the confluence with the Mago. This exploit proved to be more difficult than expected: on New Year's Day of 1896 a huge crocodile attacked one of his men. This was a bad omen, because ten days later Neumann himself was almost torn to pieces by a raging elephant. This was the last straw: after two months of painful convalescence, Neumann left the banks of the Rudolf with his haul of ivory. That same year another hardy traveler had followed Teleki's tracks. The American Donaldson Smith, coming from Somalia, had hacked and fought his way through the land of the bellicose Borana as far as Lake Chamo and

finally came within sight of Lake Stefanie. After meticulously surveying the banks of the lake, he then headed toward the Omo, determined to verify whether it was indeed the famous Nianam that Teleki had described. Donaldson Smith followed the route for about one hundred miles; once past the locality of Karo, the river narrowed gradually until it became a rapids about 66 feet wide. He therefore deduced that the source could not be far off, perhaps beyond the mountain chain that crowned the valley. Therefore the Niaman could not possibly be the Omo. Actually, Donaldson Smith, searching for a way out of the labyrinth of marshes fronting the Mago, had gone back up the course of the tributary, deceived by the narrow curve that the Omo makes in a southwesterly direction. Instead of being untangled, the matter had become even more confused.

The question of the Omo was by then the last enigma in African geography. At any rate, this was the opinion of Vittorio Bottego, an officer in the Italian Army. Blessed with the unusual combination of a hardy constitution, reckless nature, and dogged determination, Bottego also had a first-rate knowledge of botany, zoology, geology and cartography. His capacities had already been tested during an earlier voyage of exploration to the sources of the Juba River, during which he had won the esteem of the new Italian Geographic Society and the admiration of numerous persons, so that his goal to solve once and for all the problem of the Omo immediately attracted attention. Bottego's plan was quite clear: he intended to reach the course of the river at the same point Borelli had left over 15 years before and from there follow it to its mouth, wherever that might be. On 12 October 1895 the expedition, comprising hundreds of men and 160 pack animals

The Karo village of Korcho offers a majestic view of the Omo River.

left the desolate coast of southern Somalia and headed to the interior. Six months later the men arrived within sight of Lake Abaya, one of the seven natural basins dotting the bottom of the Rift Valley in Ethiopia. Accurate reconnaissance excluded the theory that the Abaya, which Bottego called the Margherita, had any relation whatsoever with the waters of the Omo. There was nothing else to do but continue the march through the impervious mountains that extended to the west. As the caravan penetrated farther and farther into the plateau, the Ethiopians became more and more hostile. Only three months earlier, unbeknown to Bottego, the Italian troops had suffered a crushing defeat at Adwa. The Ethiopian forts on the Kaffa frontier were hostile to foreigners: attacks were constant, resulting in many dead and wounded on both sides. Because of the overwhelming odds against them, the explorers found themselves in a desperate plight, yet Bottego did not abandon his plans and forged ahead at top speed toward his goal. On 29 June 1896 the majestic and wild Omo suddenly appeared behind the last row of trees. The explorers could not restrain their joy and excitement: "We stood there, astonished, silent, to contemplate that unknown region that fantasy had so many times, in thousands of ways, portrayed for us and that now stretched before us in all its solemn reality."

Astronomic bearings confirmed the latitude of 6°43: from that point on, the course of the river was completely unknown. In order to avoid ambushes on the part of the Ethiopians, Bottego decided to abandon the forests of the valley line and climb up the mountains again. This was a difficult time with sleepless nights

after three weeks, Bottego and his men came to a vast grassy plain where the Omo, taking in the waters of the Dinchia, heads southward. The explorers followed its winding course and arrived in a marshy area. Repeating the mistake made by Donaldson Smith, Bottego headed into the Mago River valley with determination, but soon found that that limpid rapids had nothing at all to do with the Omo River. They discovered the mouth of the river a week later. The spectacle that lay before the Italians from the top of a low hill left no room for doubt: the Omo slowly flowed in the jade-colored waters of Lake Rudolf, ruffled by a slight breeze. "From this moment on," Bottego wrote, "the great problem of modern geography has been solved and our dream has been realized."

An excursion to Lake Stefanie yielded a large quantity of ivory, which was added to that already accumulated. Maurizio Sacchi, one of Bottego's three lieutenants, was ordered to return to the base in Lugh, Somalia, to put the ivory in a safe place. But unfortunately things turned out differently: on the way to Lake Abaya Sacchi's party fell victim to a surprise attack on the part of a group of Amhara robbers. Sacchi died during the skirmish, but Bottego never found out about it. Intoxicated by success, he was determined to carry out his mission. The fact that the Omo flowed into Lake Rudolf was of capital importance,

but it did not exclude the existence of a distributary, perhaps connected to the upper Sobat and hence the White Nile. The eastern shore had already been carefully explored by Teleki, Neumann and Donaldson Smith, but no one had yet set foot on the western shore. On November 5 the expedition crossed the river, which was 720 feet and up to 20 feet deep at some points. It took several days of tribulation to ford the river. Leaving the last Dhaasanac villages behind him, Bottego followed the shore of the lake up to the mouth of the Turkwel, on a line with the present-day city of Lodwar, in Kenya. The search for possible distributaries was fruitless. No river flowed out of Lake Rudolf. Satisfied with his successful venture, Bottego could have backtracked along paths he knew, but he decided to head north toward the Sobat and the heart of the Ethiopian Empire.

On the road to Adis Abeba the caravan was attacked by Ethiopians. Bottego died during the battle and two of his comrades, Vannutelli and Citerni, were shackled. After 90 days they were set free, and miraculously managed to return to Italy safe and sound. Their memoirs, together with the naturalist collections that had survived the disaster, provided the first certain information concerning the local populations, the geography, fauna and flora of the region. The secrets of the Omo River had been revealed forever.

45 The Galeb at Omorate have marked features and a distressed look.

46-47 In the village of Korcho, a family listens intently to a discussion taking place outside their hut.

48-49 Surma children in the village of Kormu burn the brush in order to plant sorghum

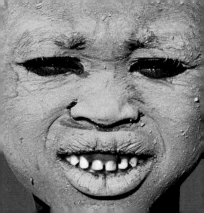

THE HEIRS OF TUMU

THE SURMA

INNOCENT WARRIORS

[PAOLO NOVARESIO]

THE SURMA

INNOCENT WARRIORS

ON HIGH, IN THE DEPTHS OF THE DARK BLUE SKY, IS TUMU, THE SUPREME GOD, WHO IS THE MASTER OF RAIN, WHICH SUDDENLY FILLS THE PARCHED RIVERBEDS AND INJECTS NEW LIFE INTO THE FIELDS AND OFFERS RELIEF TO THE THIRSTY ANIMALS.

Tumu is remote and mysterious: neither songs nor prayers and invocations are addressed to him, nor can one get to know him after death, which is the end of everything. The Ancestors are also indifferent to human destiny: they are remembered for their glorious achievements but are not venerated.

The Surma know they have to manage by themselves, day by day. Not even Islam or Christianity has influenced their pragmatic conception of human existence. Indifferent to religion, lacking an organized power system, self-sufficient, they live isolated in the wild mountains covered with forests and savannas. Their oral tradition tells us that they originated in the lower Omo River valley, north of Lake Turkana, but their language seems to indicate they are of Nilotic descent. The Surma vehemently deny any relationship whatsoever with the Mursi and Meen, despite the fact that have similar customs and speak the same tongue. But another pop-

ulation belongs to their group: the Bale, who live in the Akobo river region, between Sudan and Ethiopia. The only notable difference between the Bale and the Surma, properly speaking, is the possession of livestock. The former have been farmers for generations, while the Surma proudly consider themselves herdsmen, even though they are also forced to till the land. In fact, in the 1970s an epidemic of blackleg wiped out their herds, causing great hardship, and in order to survive the Surma began to plant sorghum and corn.

However, the Surma's system of values has remained intact: cows continue to be considered symbols of wealth, nobility and social status. The sale of gold, which is relatively abundant in this zone, provides the means to purchase other animals. The Surma discovered that gold could also be used to buy firearms and ammunition from nearby Sudan, which is in a perpetual state of civil war. The guns made it easier to acquire livestock and the raids on their age-old enemies, the Nyangatom, increased in number. For about twenty years the Surma have been at war with their southern neighbor: attacks and retaliation are the rule, with considerable loss of life on both sides. The former balance of power

Undulating white marks decorate the face and body of this proud Surma.

with the Dizi and the other neighboring peoples has also been upset, and intertribal tension is very high.

The insecurity that reigns in the region, which has no communication routes, discourages intervention on the part of the government: the Surma are formally under the authority of the state, but really enjoy political autonomy, do not pay taxes and run their affairs without any external interference. In reality the Surma territory has never really been conquered. It was annexed to the Ethiopian Empire in 1897 and passed under Italian dominion a few decades later, without anything really changing. The Communist regime of Haile Mengistu Mariam fared no better. To this day, the Surma villages can be reached only on foot, on narrow paths that are almost blocked by the thick vegetation. There are no roads, schools or hospitals.

The hills between the Kibish River and the scarp that descends to the Omo River valley constitute one of the most remote and inaccessible areas in the African continent. The rainfall, about 600 mm per year, comes in spring and summer in violent showers. During the dry season the average temperature is never below 33 °C and in the lowlands, infested by tsetse flies, the heat is unbearable.

Protected by this harsh, impenetrable environment, the Surma have preserved their ancient customs. The last census accounted for about 20,000 persons, listed as Suri and divided into the Chai and Tirma subgroups. Surma society is organized in clans, based on the age-group principle. Those belonging to the same family are not obliged to live together but can move about and choose their residence freely. Despite this, the clan is characterized by strong internal solidarity that comes to the fore during moments of crisis and during ceremonies.

Strict rules establish the line of inheritance: the assets of the deceased are divided into shares that take into account the ages of the children. The first-born inherits the best animals and most precious objects, first and foremost the guns, usually Kalashnikovs or M-16s. The other heirs must make do with old muskets and the few things left over.

The elders are highly respected, as are their opinions: they always have the last word in the meetings, which they direct. However, the opinions expressed are not binding and the individual's freedom to decide for himself is never disputed.

The Surma have no chiefs as such. Ethnologists describe this type of social organism as headless or segmented, since there is no centralized political structure able to impose its will through coercion. The basic unit in this society is the family, consisting of the wife and her children; the men, usually polygamous, carry out most of their tasks far from home. Besides defending their land, the men take care of the livestock, which are kept in enclosures near the pastureland, which may be even more than a day's walk from the village. Hunting wild animals, including large ones, is a major source of food. Poaching in the nearby Omo National Park is common practice.

The women take care of the crops and everything else in domestic life. They tan the hides and also make lovely pottery that is both used at home and sold on the market or traded for basic necessities. Their economic self-sufficiency and the rather vague moral norms allow them a certain degree of liberty. Sexual

This woman shows her large labret, which in this area may also have a semicircular shape.

intercourse before marriage is rather common and the mothers make sure to teach their daughters the ins and outs of courtship and lovemaking, suggesting the best way to avoid pregnancy.

The Surma hold physical beauty and grooming in high esteem, and body painting is of the utmost aesthetic importance. As is the case with the Mursi, together with the glass bead necklaces and metal bracelets, lip ornaments are part of a woman's seductive repertoire. The labret, made of wood or clay and either round or trapezoidal, may have a large diameter.

The taste for decking-out the body is best expressed during the celebrations held at harvest time at the end of the rain season. On this occasion the men engage in bloody duels with poles, showing off their strength and manliness, and the girls choose their future husbands from among the contenders. Later, the families, after patient negotiations that may last months, set the wedding date and decide upon amount of the dowry in animals and guns. The ceremony, which is in effect a pact of alliance between the two families, is accompanied by beer, songs and dances. Lastly, the bride solemnly enters the new hut that her spouse has prepared for her. And the warm evening bids farewell to the fascinating, primeval world of the Surma.

[GIANNI GIANSANTI]

THE SURMA

KORMU, THE TIMELESS VILLAGE

IT'S OUR LAST NIGHT AT KORMU. TOMORROW WE SET OFF AGAIN. I WONDER IF I'LL EVER SEE THESE PEOPLE AGAIN. A QUESTION THAT IS ALMOST SENTIMENTAL AND CERTAINLY UNUSUAL FOR ME, SINCE I'VE LIVED HERE ONLY FIVE DAYS.

However, time and its duration lose their objective value and take on emotional value related to the intensity of one's experience: five days together with them, in their homes, and with the rhythm of a vanishing world, changes one's normal perception of the flow of events.

Tomorrow we will leave and I would like to reciprocate for the hospitality I have received with a memory, an experience, an emotion – in other words, something that cannot be purchased. The moonlight highlights the contours. Everything else is total darkness. Yesterday the Kormu children watched me select some digital photographs on the computer and they were flabbergasted. "This spectacle shouldn't be only for a few people, let's show it to everybody!" This may be the very gift I'm looking for. Fassil helps me to speak with the village chief and explain that it would be my pleasure to invite the children to watch me at work at my table in the evening after supper. My invitation elicits curiosity and agitation. The supper is brief and silent; all the while

we can hear the chatter of the Surma who are a few feet distant, but they did not come to see, touch, and ask questions as they usually do. In the almost total darkness that pervades beyond the rays of light of the camp lamp there are only words without a face or direction: whispers of those who do not want to disturb, the waiting and expectation of those who want to see? It is obvious that they know what respect means. A gesture suffices to make the voices become persons; in the darkness I can barely make out movements. There are not only children, the entire village has come. The father of the chief sits next to me and asks for the usual cigarette with the usual glance; between us there's no need for words. In the outdoor movie theater smoking is allowed....

The scene that unfolds is delightful.

On one side – with a noisy, aggressive, warlike temperament – the members of an entire Surma village stand in orderly fashion around a field table in front of the computer display to look at my photographs to the rhythm of music. The Surma laugh and sigh in disbelief, cover their faces with their hands in amazement, sometimes in fright, when on the screen, once the photographs have been shown, the animated effects of iTunes dance before their eyes.

On the other side, we who are used to the

Spurred by curiosity, a Surma looks into the lens, using a roll as an earring.

photographs, enjoy this spectacle with the spectacle: shining eyes; teeth that are very white or appear so by contrast; hands in front of faces; the black with blue nuances because of the light from the monitor; voices so shrill they seem unreal that laugh, shout, and comment, that recognize the Mursi and mistake the Hamer for the Benna and vice versa, that make fun of the Harborè, God knows why.... Every-body is laughing and happy except for the chief guard, who has been suspicious from the mo-ment the music began. He talks to Fassil, ask-ing or ordering something. Fassil breaks out in-to laughter and translates for us: "He said to stop, bekha, and asked me, "Where is the man who is singing?" All around, the moonlight marks out the edges of a village that lies be-yond time. Beyond my time, even beyond the darkness. At this hour the streets along the Tiber in Rome are blocked by traffic.

Standing on a rock, this man is scanning the horizon; he can see as far as the Magologni hot springs.

Welè Ghida, hunter from
Kormu, mounts a search
with his Kalashnikov.

Sorghum, or life

The brown gold of the Surma

65

The Surma children's day begins
by gathering sorghum.

Kormu

In the heart of the Omo Valley

The Surma village of Kormu, which numbers about thirty domed huts, at dawn. At the entrance to the village is a clearing where meetings are held.

68-69 Scenes of everyday life in Kormu:
the women, with their children, intent on
preparing food.

69 Sorghum, both milled and in grains, is the
basic element not only of the Surma economy,
but also of their diet.

For the children, every aspect of village life is experienced
in a sort of wild freedom, as they live together with the grazing
animals they look after.

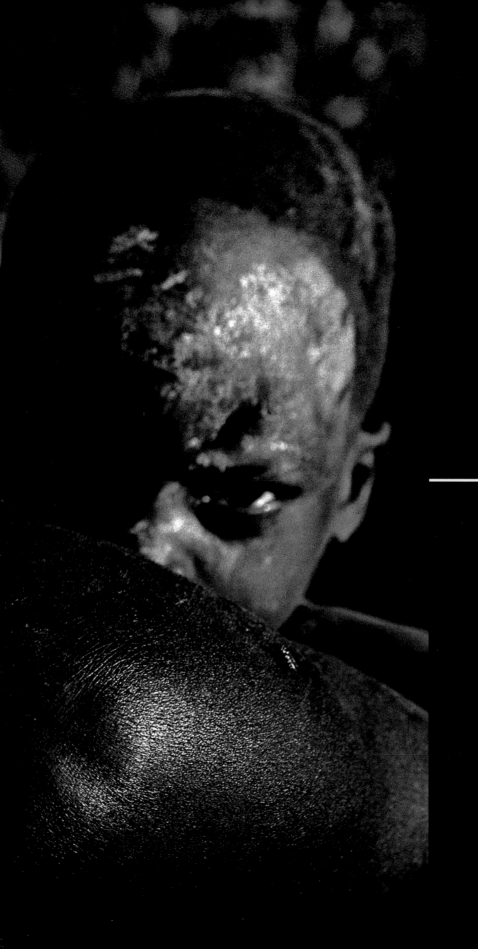

A woman with a large labret
carries her son on her back.

Besides wearing labrets, the Surma,
like the Mursi, also pierce and widen
their ear lobes in order to insert
wooden disks in them.
These women have decorated their heads
with colored berries for a celebration.

These Surma children add the finishing touch to
their body painting with floral decoration.

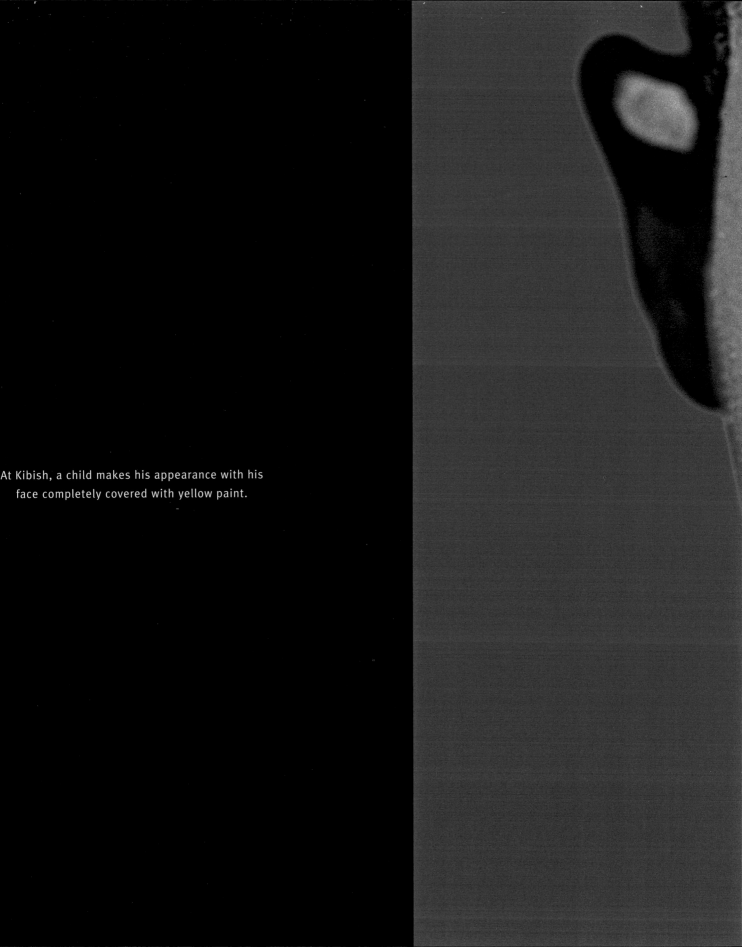

At Kibish, a child makes his appearance with his
face completely covered with yellow paint.

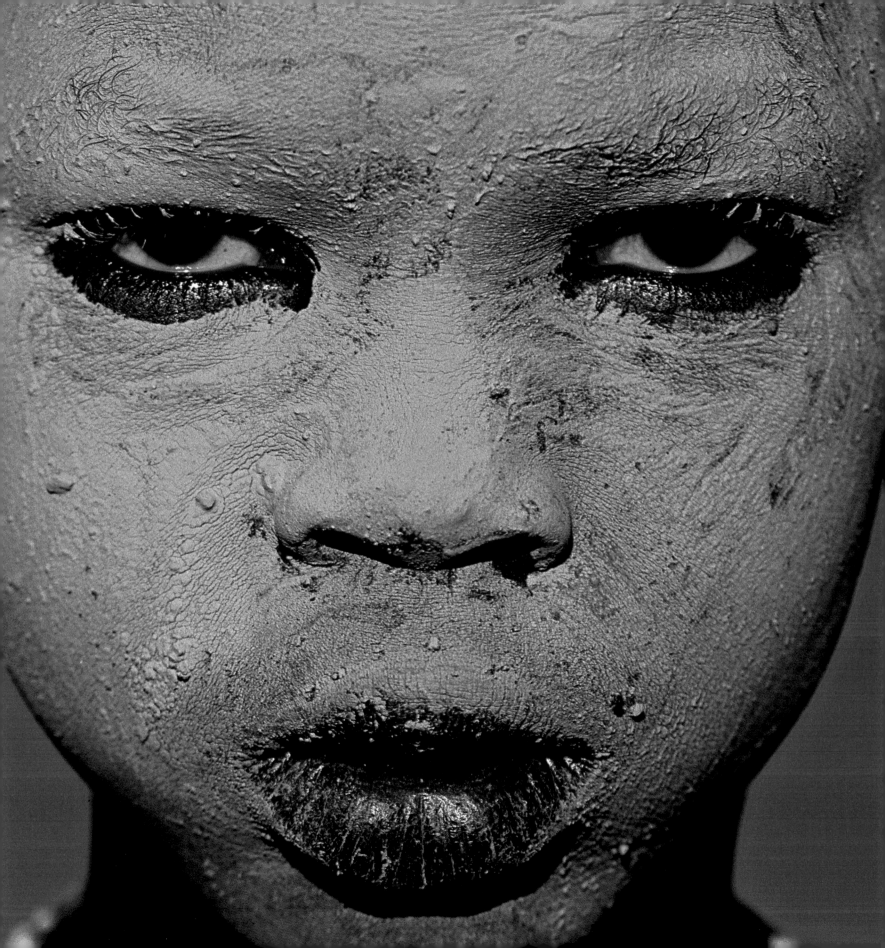

ETHIOPIA 2003/04
"OMO VALLEY"

...TOGETHER WITH
THE GLASS BEAD
NECKLACES AND
METAL BRACELETS,
LIP ORNAMENTS ARE
PART OF A WOMAN'S
SEDUCTIVE REPERTOIRE.

80 The size of the labret is a sign of the woman's beauty: the larger the labret, the more desirable the woman is considered.

82 This Surma boy from Kormu adorned his face with simple dabs of white made of chalk and water.

83 All the children of Kormu perform a sort of dance consisting of skips and hops, accompanied by a song they sing while clapping their hands.

84, 85 and 86-87 The children also compete with one another in decorating their bodies, which at times leads to the creation of works made of mud or clay to be placed on the head

SCARIFICATION
MARKS OF HONOR

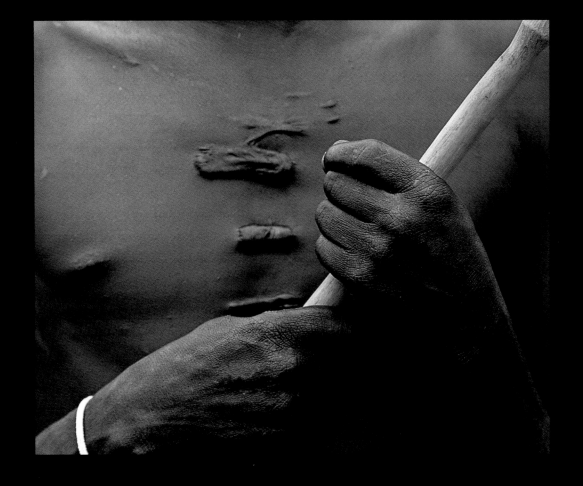

88 This man's expression seems to summarize all the characteristics of the Surma people.

89 The Surma warrior Wollechibo shows the scars he got during the Donga, the traditional combat with poles.

A Surma girl expert in this custom, is absorbed
in carving scars on the arm of a young man.

The scars on men arms should indicate the number of enemies killed

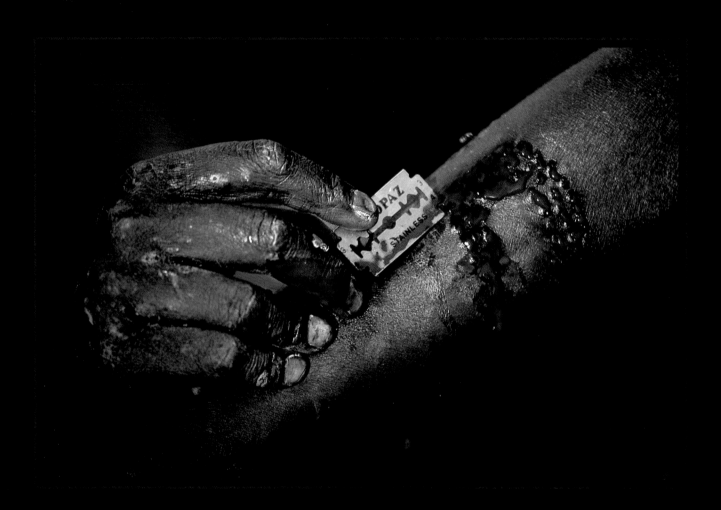

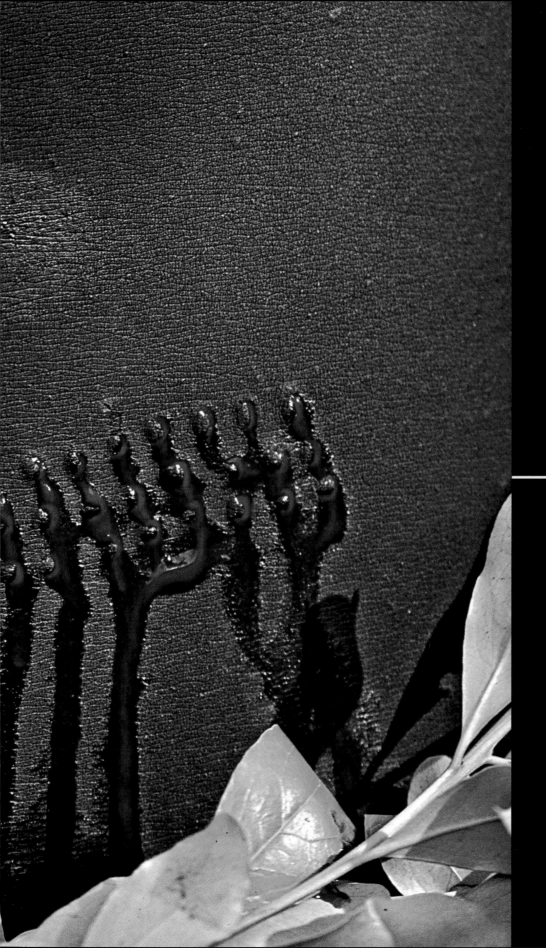

The women have scars on their arms,
shoulders, breasts and, above all,
stomach. The Surma are true masters in
the art of scarification, a practise that is
carried out without any attention or
haste: the blood flows freely from the
wound and is cleaned with leaves.

The Magologni hot springs are also frequented by girls, who are seen here decorating one another's hair.

Before creating abstract patterns, the men
wash one another thoroughly at the springs.

Magologni

The sources of color

The hot springs of Magologni are one of the
main places where the Surma go to do their
body painting.

Having taken off their clothes and put down their Kalashnikovs, the Surma begin to paint their bodies white. The painting has no particular symbolic meaning, but serves as a mark of distinction to attract women and also to intimidate their enemies in battle.

Together with body painting, the other decorative element of the Surma, and of the other Omo Valley ethnic groups in general, is their hairdo. Here a man is carefully cutting another man's hair and shaving him with *mellachi* blades.

In general, unmarried
men are very meticulous
about their body painting,
which will make them
fascinating and original in
the eyes of the women.

Abstract patterns that look like real masterpieces in motion
become alive on the statuesque bodies of the Surma people.

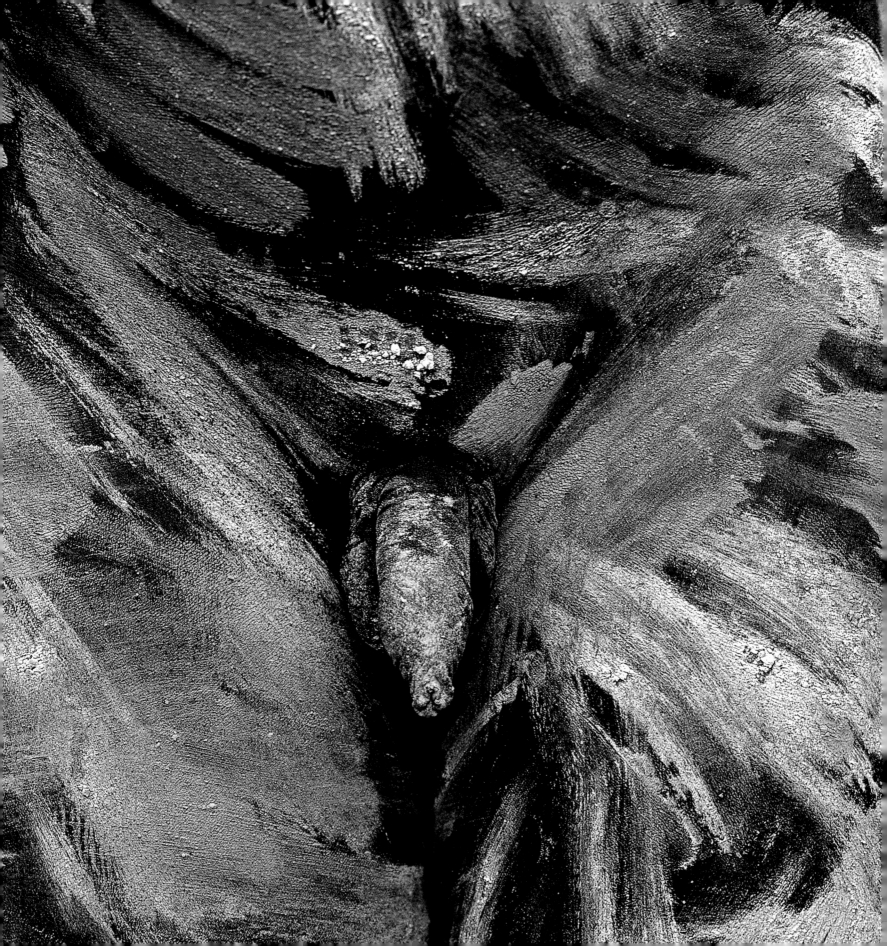

Men painting themselves with a color obtained from a sort of plaster mixed with water.

The motifs of the body painting have
no particular symbolic meaning,
but rather they follow the rules of
taste and tradition.

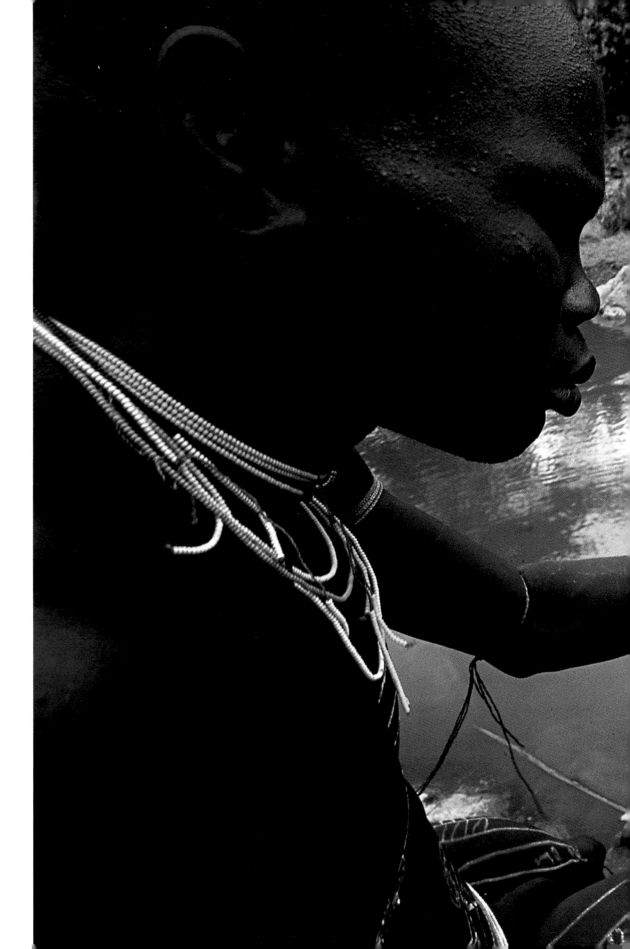

The colors used for body painting are obtained by rubbing wet stones against one another.

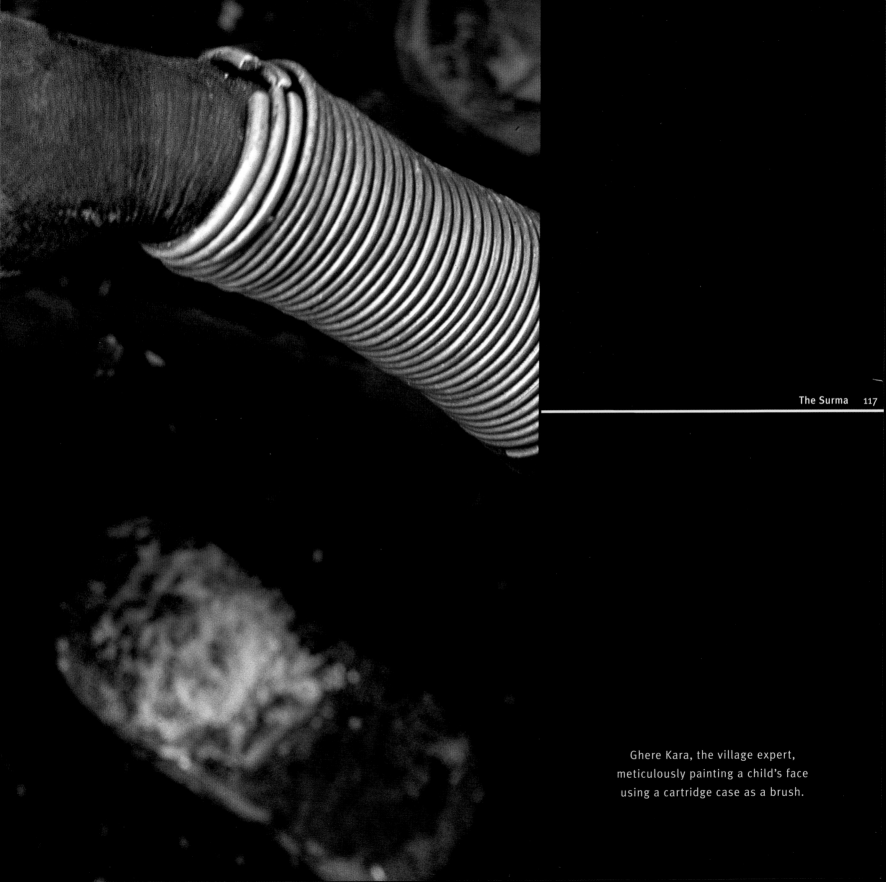

Ghere Kara, the village expert,
meticulously painting a child's face
using a cartridge case as a brush.

118-119 A war mask: the
red marks, here painted
with the aid of a stick, are
intended to intimidate
the enemy.

120-121 A village near
Tulgit is the venue for the
Zigroo, the lip-piercing
ceremony.
It is the custom among the
Surma to make an incision
in the lower lip of the
women/girls in order to
insert the labret. When
the wound heals, they
hold the Zigroo festivities,
with all the villagers
participating.

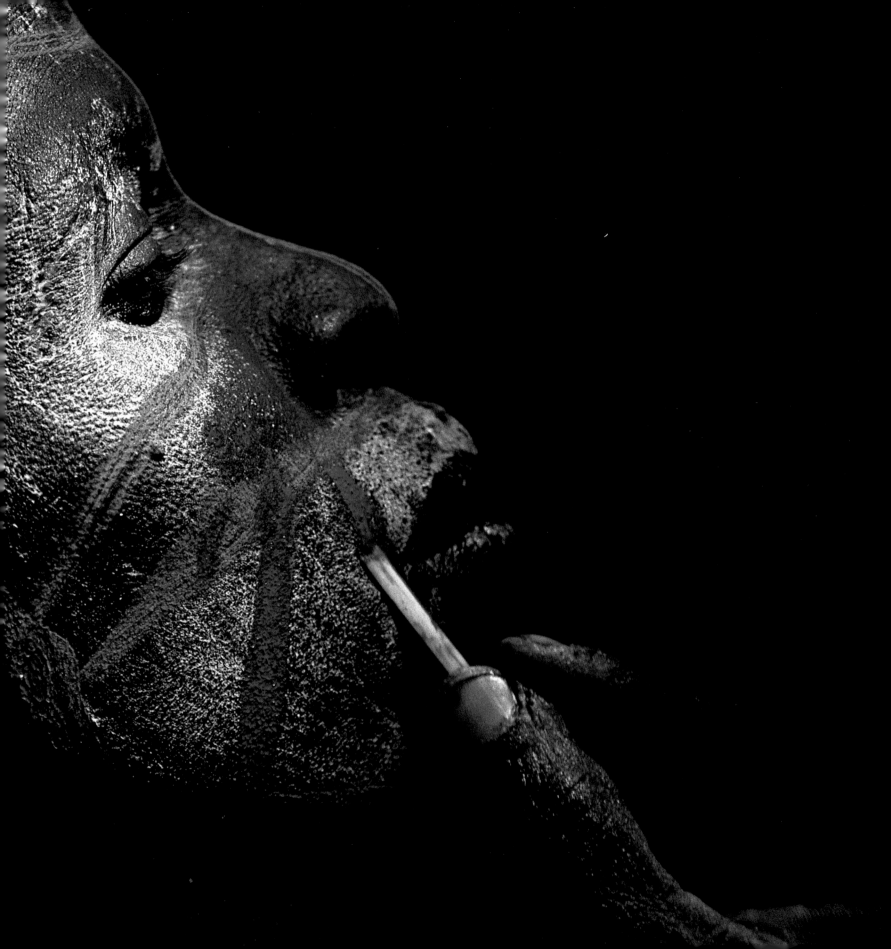

During the festivities,
some people go off to
drink beer made from
fermented cereals.

Surma men and women celebrate with
dances and songs, which are
interrupted by Kalashnikov shots every
time a woman from a neighboring
village sets, in a pre-established place,
a leather bag filled with beer offered
for the occasion.

The dances last for several
hours and everyone
participates, including,
naturally, the women whose
lips have been cut.

128-129 Leaning on their poles, three
boys observe their friends, who
are dancing frenziedly.

130-131 The men hold onto their
Kalashnikovs even during the dance,
pointing them directly at the crowd.

The Blood Meal

A primeval ritual

The Blood Meal is one of the propitiatory rituals of the
Surma, a tribe of farmers and livestock breeders who
entrust their hopes for survival to their animals.

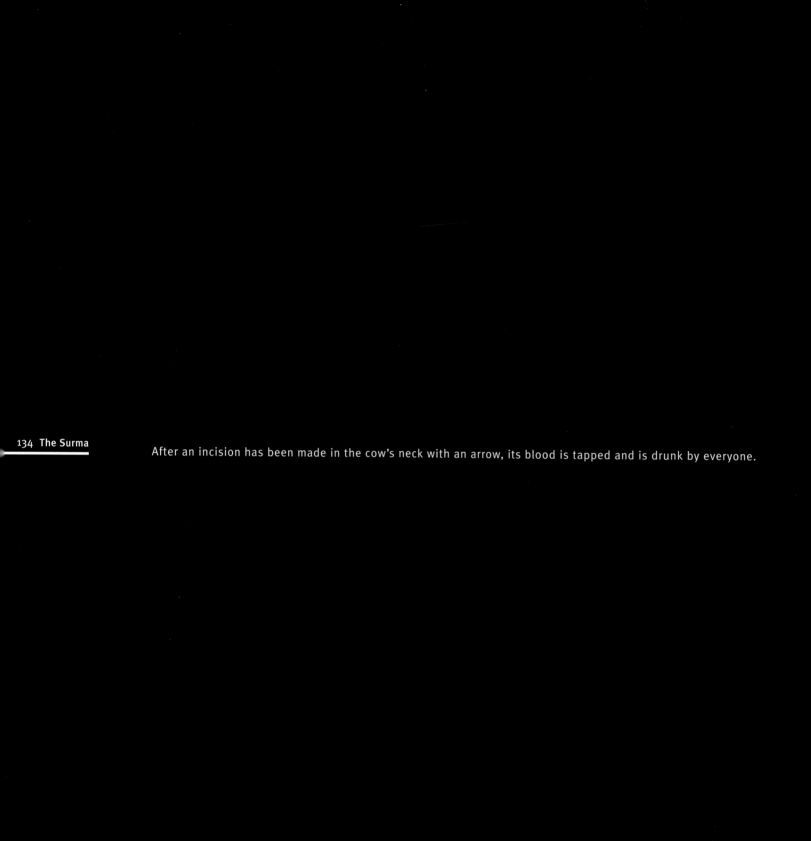

After an incision has been made in the cow's neck with an arrow, its blood is tapped and is drunk by everyone.

The Blood Meal is cruel, but the
animal must not be killed, since it
is a source of wealth for the entire
tribe. The incision is really a small
wound that will heal as soon as
the ritual is over.

The Blood Meal exemplifies the Surmas' relationship with nature, which is considered essential to life

[GIANNI GIANSANTI]

THE DONGA

POLE COMBAT

W E'RE GOING TO WATCH, FILM AND TAKE PHOTOGRAPHS OF THE DONGA RITUAL, ONE OF WHICH IS CELEBRATED IN A VILLAGE THREE HOURS' WALK FROM TULGIT, SO THEY SAY. HOWEVER, WE'VE GOT TO GET MOVING, BECAUSE IT'S ALREADY TWO O'CLOCK AND THE DONGA − NOT THE DONGA IN ITSELF, BUT ALL ITS REPERCUSSIONS − BEGINS TO GET DANGEROUS AFTER FOUR O'CLOCK.

At that hour the people, armed with Kalashnikovs, start to drink, lose control, and when they are all drunk they shoot into the air − and it seems that some of them are very poor shots. Everything's ready; let's get going! In that quarter of an hour we come upon a group of Surma who ask for a ride. "Walk there," we reply. "After all, for you fellows it's no strain, you're used to it." The boys don't get angry; quite the contrary, they take us by the hand. "Chally, chally," they smile. One the them, who must be over six feet tall, with a cane in his hand, a dreamy expression on his face and small, round sunglasses (who knows where he stole them), continues to say goodbye: "Chally, chally." Right after this our car gets bogged down in the mud, so we also have to go all the way on foot, up exhausting ascents and over interminable mountains. We go up and down one, two, three

hills and they continue to tell us that the peak we are looking for is the next one. When we arrive at the village, after four o'clock, the Donga has already begun some time ago. This is the Donga: the entire village assembles in a circle in a clearing, where the combat, a duel with poles, takes place, and after every battle the winner is challenged by another person, and so forth. Every so often they stop and sing. Before the combat begins the village chief gives orders and instructions. There are few rules, perhaps only one: do not kill your opponent. There are no rich prizes for the winner, but he earns the esteem of the whole village, is considered valorous, and is appreciated by the girls. In this part of the world, this is quite a lot.... What we are watching is a true Donga, not those organized for tourists. The situation seems tense, everybody has drunk a lot, blood is spattered everywhere and the blows are quite violent. All around come cries of pain and encouragement, bloodied faces and eyes filled with anger threaten me every time I lift up my camera. The Surma in the circle move backward when the combatants get near them, in order to avoid the occasional wild blow. Noise, furious blows, ominous Kalashnikovs, blood, cries, pain, threatening savage looks, chaos. Until suddenly silence reigns. Every-

141 left With this makeshift head guard, one of the contenders gets ready for the duel.

141 right The Donga ritual is not a dance, but combat that brings both wounds and honor to both the winner and loser.

body stops and turns around. On the path to the village are the inhabitants from a nearby village who have come to challenge this one. They are lined up in a triangle. In the first row is the man with little sunglasses whom we had met before; then he looked absent-minded, but now he seems the image of the pride and daring typical of warriors. Behind him are his fellow townspeople, first two, then three, and so on, forming the triangle. They stop for just a second and then, all together, raise their poles to the sound of a cry: this is a sign of a challenge. It all looks like the scene in a motion picture. Everything happens with the same studied and rational procedures and tempo of the cinema, not the apparently casual events of reality. There is the most deafening uproar and then absolute silence, and, once again, that proud glance and battle cry. One village challenges another one. The combat now becomes a political affair: formerly it was a question of personal honor, now one fights for the community. The adversaries, under the aegis of their chief, win. One is borne in triumph and everybody begins to drink, sing, dance, shoot. For us it is really becoming too dangerous, so we set off. On the way back we hear the voices and Kalashnikov shots for quite some time, then nothing more. In front of us are only the interminable mountains.

Wearing a sort of waistcoat
and cloth headdress, and
holding their poles, these
young warriors are ready to
begin a Donga combat.

The Donga training takes place in a clearing near the village, and the combatants fight in earnest.

Their bodies are decorated with ritual drawings and their heads are protected by a sort of helmet of plants interwoven with colored cotton. For the boys who participate in the Donga with their ritual painting and head guards, this challenge is a true moment of glory.

THE DUEL

WITH POLES

From 148 to 153 In the middle of a
circle made by the crowd,
the Donga combatants begin to swipe
at one another. The rules are simple
and can be summed up as follows: the
person who manages to stay on his feet
is the winner, and one absolutely must
not kill his opponent.

Wounded and smeared with blood, the exhausted contenders watch the final duels. The winner will be nored by the entire tribe, while the loser will wait for his wounds to heal and try again at the next Donga.

THE
BUME

MAN HUNTERS

[PAOLO NOVARESIO]

THE BUME

MAN HUNTERS

I

N ITS LAST STRETCH, BEFORE REACHING
LAKE TURKANA, THE OMO RIVER CROSSES ONE
OF THE MOST REMOTE AREAS IN ETHIOPIA.

The arid land that extends past the right bank of the river toward the unstable frontiers with Sudan and Kenya are inhabited by populations of semi-nomadic herdsmen, in constant strife among one another. A report written in the early 1930s for the British Foreign Office describes those desolate lands as "completely useless, unproductive and unable to support any population." This is followed by a list of horrors: "The water is practically non-existent, the pastures poor. The heat is intense and there is no shade. The entire country is an expanse of thorny bushes, dry grass and muddy plains." The colonial powers divided the territory among themselves by merely looking at maps, without bothering to notice that the borders they were drawing up actually lay over an already existing geometric pattern. An invisible network of transhumance tracks, which changed according to the seasons, already divided the tribal spheres of influence: for the Turkana, Toposa, Dhaasanac and Nyangatom, access to the so-called Ilemi Triangle was of crucial importance to their very survival. A series of agreements established by custom regulated co-existence among the various ethnic groups, limiting their

conflicts. For a few decades this delicate balance has been on verge of breaking down. The expansionist aims of Kenya, the war of liberation in Sudan and the availability of great quantities of modern weapons have all drastically altered what was the status quo. The Ilemi Triangle, tormented by continuous warfare, is the domain of total anarchy. The emergency is such that in the last decade the Nyangatom, harassed by the advance of the Turkana, have been forced to abandon their old migration routes and move northward, up to the edge of the Omo National Park.

The Nyangatom, 14,000 persons strong, are an ethnic group of Nilotic origin and belong to the large Karamojong group. In the list of ethnic groups in southern Ethiopia they are also called Donyiro or Dongiro, and in the Amhara language they are known as Bume. They originally came from north Uganda and settled in their present territory, between the Omo and Kibish rivers, a little more than a century ago. They have close linguistic ties with the Turkana and the Toposa of Sudan. Cattle, sheep and goat herdsmen, they also practice agriculture, and the sorghum, millet and corn they cultivate along the banks of the rivers are staples in their diet. Wild honey and above all crocodile meat are occasional but important sources of nutrition.

An intense portrait of a Bume woman.

The crocodiles that live in the Omo River are often more than 13 feet long and are among the most aggressive on the African continent. The Nyangatom capture them by lancing them with a long harpoon with a line attached to it. The hunt, which takes place on pirogues made of tree trunks, is fraught with danger and requires great skill. Nyangatom society is based on a generational system and has profound similarities with that of the Turkana. Despite the apparent hostility between these groups, they are united by strong economic ties. Trade between them concerns mostly agricultural products, livestock, pottery and ocher powder, which the groups use as a pigment to decorate their bodies. The material culture of the two groups also reveals marked similarities: both the Turkana and Nyangatom women wear leather pubertal aprons with a typical triangular shape that are often adorned with glass beads and discs made of ostrich shells. Another, larger animal hide apron hangs from their hips and covers the back of their legs. The glass beads used to make thick neckbands are very much appreciated as a symbol of fascination and elegance. An integral part of male clothing among the Nyangatom are the clay topknots or headdresses that decorate the heads of all the men when they attain a certain age. Making this headdress requires long, patient work: a mixture of earth and water is spread on the hair, layer after layer, until a perfectly smooth crown is created. While the clay is still wet, a rectangular plate made of wood or cow entrails and pierced with holes is attached to the headdress with string. This will serve as a support for the ostrich feathers that, together with red and indigo pigments, will add the final touch to this creation. Over and above its purely aesthetic value, the headdress protects the head from skin and hair parasites, as it stops them from spreading. The custom of making scars serves a parallel hygienic purpose: the Nyngatom, like the Dhaasanac, Mursi and other ethnic groups in the region, celebrate the killing of an enemy or a dangerous animal by making a series of cuts on their chests that usually form a vertical line. Inserting ashes and plant substances under the skin helps to delay the scar tissue healing, thus causing the growth of conspicuous protuberances that highlight the stature of an individual and his being part of a tribe. The cuts are made with blades, acacia thorns and other implements that are certainly not sterilized; the slow healing process makes for the formation of antibodies and acts as a kind of vaccination that helps to prevent the risk of future infections. In the pitiless world of the Nyangatom there are no certainties or guarantees; they live in the present without knowing what is in store for them in the future, which the clairvoyants try to read in cow entrails. And yet, their harsh everyday existence leaves room for festivities and ceremonies. Victories in battle, a successful raid, weddings and all major social occasions are celebrated to the ancient rhythm of the nidjeroi, metal rattles that dancers attach to their elbows and knees. The art of music and song represents the very identity of the Nyangatom, which is endangered, and their pride in feeling unique and different from others. These words and sounds travel afar, carrying their message to the land of the Dhaasanac, the Hamer and the Arbore, beyond the banks of the great river.

Glass beads, iron and shells are the basic elements of the Bume women's 'jewelry

THE BUME

THE THIRTEEN LINES

From Murulle, which was our base, we headed toward the Bume territory with the aim of finding a boat and getting to the other side of the Omo River.

When they found out about our plan, the Karo guides who had accompanied us during our stay at Murelle became as white as sheets and categorically refused to go with us, as the mere thought of going into the land of the Bume terrified them. "Bume kill Karo, Bume kill everyone." This was, in brief, the reason for their decision. Then Zinabu gave me an explanation. The Bume are a population of warriors. This is certainly nothing new in this part of the world, since everybody is a warrior here. But not only are the Bume warriors *par excellence*, they are ferocious as well. They are the only ethnic group that is everyone's enemy and that refuses any alliance.

I arrived at the Bume village one October afternoon, without a boat, without a ranger, and without my Karo guides (who had become fixtures in our group). The Bume live in a territory that has physical features similar to those in the area of the Dhaasanac and that borders the territory of the Surma, the Mursi and the Karo, with whom they are always at war, making ferocious raids against them.

They look much like the other populations I have visited, but differ in some significant features:

they have no particular body decoration or complicated headdress, but their skin is marked with scars that, quite unlike those of the Mursi, Surma and Karo, go to make up harmonious, symmetrical patterns that are fine, long and linear. I approached one of them: his eyes followed every step, every move I made. In some manner, with gestures and the few words of their language that I had learned, he got me to understand that that scarification, those signs on his body, had nothing to do with decoration, since indulging in frivolity and vanity was not part of the Bume culture. They are signs symbolizing the pedigree of the warriors: every sign indicates an enemy who has been killed. It was a great honor for a Bume man to have prominent scarification on his person, and the more signs he had tattooed on his body, the more valorous he is considered and the more respect he will have from others.

While thinking about the meaning of such scarification, I recalled something I had read a few days earlier, a phrase from Leo Frobenius' *Fables of Kordofan*: "I have killed 40 persons in my lifetime. When I am dead I will kill 40 more."

I began to take photographs of the Bume: their bodies, Kalashnikovs, the lines, those chests that spoke for themselves, much more than the few words in Amharic that we would be able to exchange.

Scarification and Kalashnikov are distinctive marks of the Bume warriors.

I never photographed their faces. I felt that showing their faces was tantamount to denouncing them, what with that admission of guilt they had tattooed on their bodies. I thought that these are warriors who live in territories in perennial conflict and who abide by atavistic laws, and my photos might create problems for them.... In any case, whether or not I was right in listening to the voice of my conscience, I took no portrait photographs of the Bume. But I did take pictures of their chests, which indeed tell the whole story.

"I have killed 40 persons in my lifetime. When I am dead I will kill 40 more." This phrase came to mind during my entire trip.

When I was about to take my leave, the man whom I had first met and who had not welcomed me, approached to say goodbye. Obviously, he did so with glances and silence, a handshake, and not one word. And while he was looking at me in the eyes I observed his chest. I counted the lines on it: thirteen.

"All enemies?" I asked.

"No, wild animals, too", he replied.

"Ah. Good...."

164-165 In the village of Nyangadam,
a man displays his scarification, while
other men are talking in the shade.
Each row of carving indicates an enemy
or ferocious animal he has killed.

166-167 The Bume have always been
warriors: they buy Kalashnikovs from
nearby Sudan, paying 300 *bir* or a cow
for each one.

Meat and corn

The warrior's meal

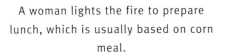

A woman lights the fire to prepare lunch, which is usually based on corn meal.

Kid goat meat is highly appreciated, and it is often the only source of proteins in the Bume diet.

Besides the glass bead necklaces, Bume women
normally wear a showy iron ring under their chins.

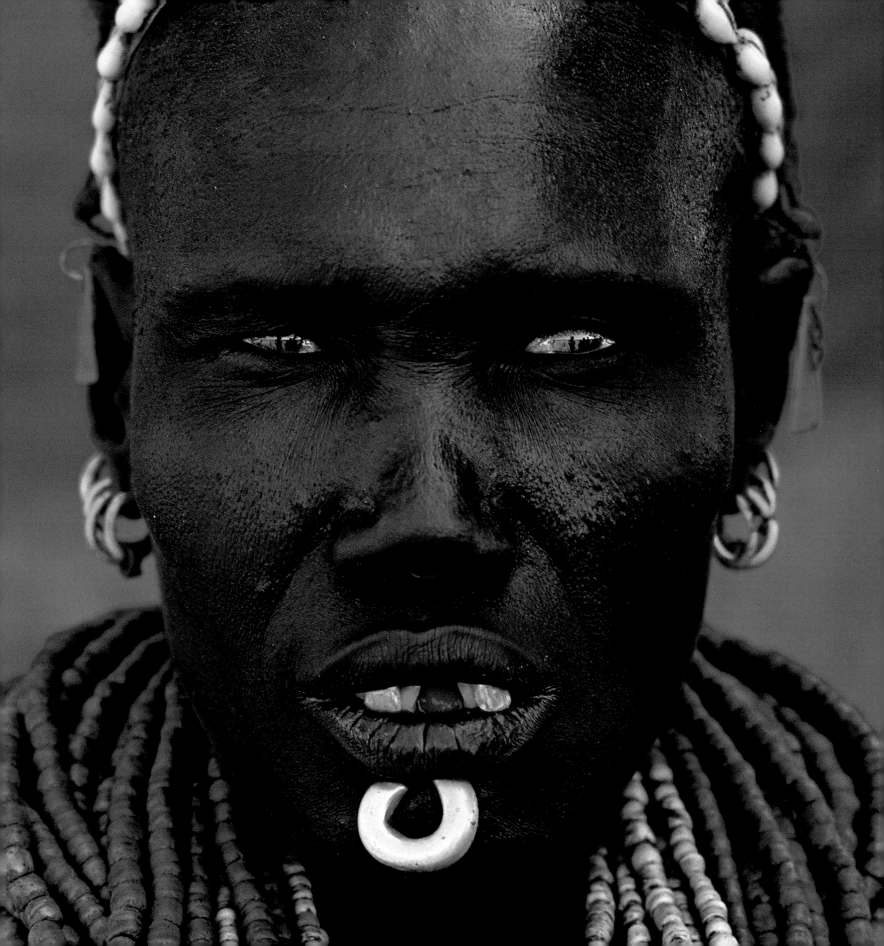

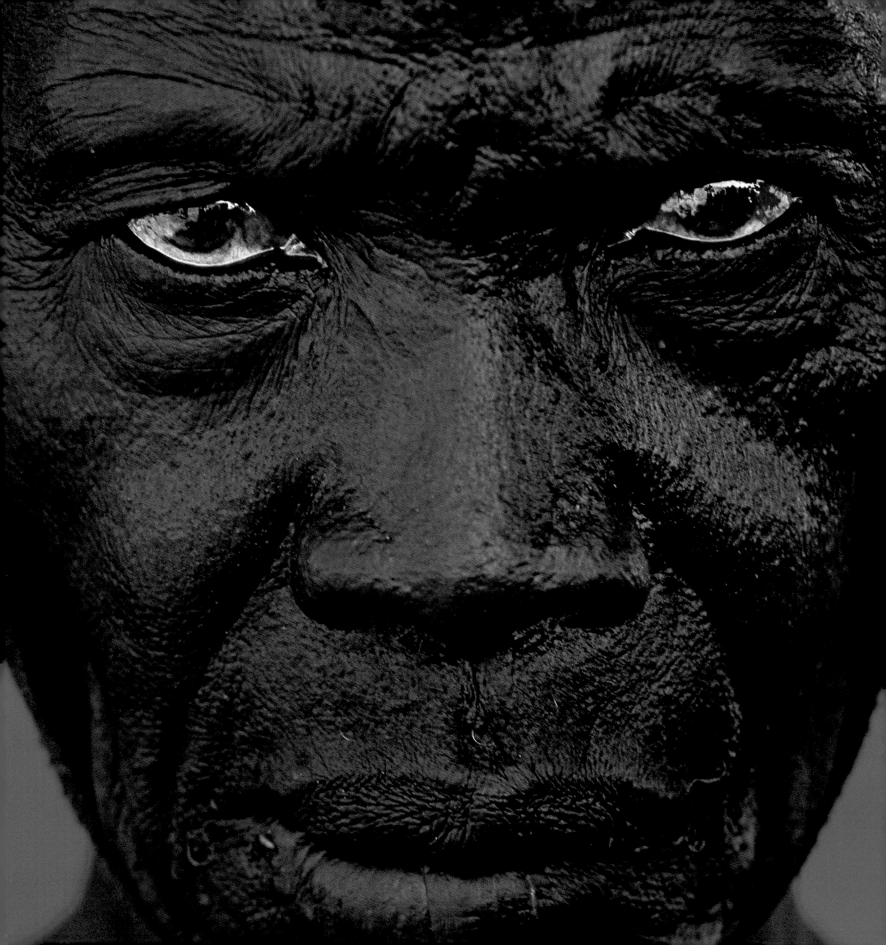

The ferocious look of the warriors sometimes results from their having eaten *chat* or hot red pepper, their drug.

THE MURSI

THE ART OF COMBAT

THE MURSI

THE ART OF COMBAT

"THESE SAVAGE TRIBES HAVE DETESTABLE TENDENCIES AND BESTIAL HABITS, AND YET THEY DO NOT DISPLAY A FEROCIOUS DISPOSITION NOR ARE THEY AS BELLICOSE AS THE MOUNTAIN DWELLERS; HOWEVER, THEIR FAMILIARITY WITH THE WOODS FOR THEIR AMBUSHES AND THEIR INSTINCTIVE MALICE MAKE THEM BOLD THIEVES INDEED."

This is the Bottego expedition's description of the Mursi (then known as Murzù), whom they met during the descent toward Lake Turkana in August 1896. The maps drawn up by Teleki and Donaldson Smith a few years earlier locates them much farther south, past the right bank of the Omo River. Since that time, continuous migration and conflicts with the neighboring tribes have forced the Mursi to settle in their present-day land, which extends north of the huge bend the Omo makes before flowing into the Mago River. This region, a hilly plateau at an altitude of about 3,280 feet, dominates the unhealthy plains of the Mago National Park. Malaria and tripanosomiasis, the sleeping sickness transmitted by the tsetse fly, discourage stable settlements on the valley floor and along the riversides. Moreover, the intense exploitation of the pastureland has transformed vast stretches of the prairie into thick, spiny scrub that is impenetrable for both man and beasts. In this merciless environment, competition for the natural resources is keen and systematic plundering becomes an indispensable survival strategy. The Mursi, who number only a little more than 3,000, are in a permanent state of war with the Bodi and Hamer, who in turn are rivals between themselves and are constantly menaced by the Nyangatom. Hundreds of warriors die in every battle. Alliances, betrayal and sudden raids follow one another in quick succession and continuously, in keeping with a mentality that gives priority to immediate advantage and self-interest. Side by side with spears and deadly wrist knives, for some time the Mursi have been using guns, from antiquated muskets used during the Italian occupation to more sophisticated repeaters.

Tourists and their cameras are tolerated only because they are a source of easy money; this is extorted in short order and used to purchase weapons and ammunition. The Mursi are fearless and awesome combatants: murder, if committed outside the tribe, is considered a virtue and honor. Showy horseshoe-shape scars ornate the men's limbs, each one symbolizing the death of an enemy. What with the violent atmosphere in this region, the most valorous warriors soon use up all the available space and the sinister decoration is then placed on every part of their bodies. Relations between the Mursi and the neighboring Kwegu, a small

A Mursi warrior with a gaudy ivory bracelet grips his faithful companion, a Soviet-made assault rifle.

ethnic group of farmer-hunters, are totally different. The latter have no animals but acknowledge their value; cows are an important component of the bride-price. The animals are provided by the Mursi, who are also responsible for the wedding negotiations and the protection of the Kwegu. In exchange the latter offer a range of services: not only do they provide honey and game meat, but also see to transportation on the river, having earned the title of "guardians of the pirogues."

At first glance the Kwegu would seem to be subjects of their guardians, without whose benevolence they would not even be able to marry. But the reality of their relationship is much more complex and articulated. Both groups play a vital role in the well-being of the community, benefiting reciprocally from this relationship, without impairing their respective identities. Intransigent with regard to intruders and proud of its isolation, Mursi society enjoys relative harmony. Disputes and problems are discussed in animated meetings that are usually held outdoors, in the shade of a large tree near the village. Anyone can speak and express his opinion. The art of public speaking is highly appreciated and the meetings often turn into spectacles of rhetoric and dramatic art. The elders, who are respected for their experience and wisdom, give the final opinion and judgment. The exuberance of the youths, who are so anxious to display their virility, is given free rein in the ritual duels between peers that take place in certain periods of the year. The best known of these tournaments, which are also common among the Surma, is the Donga, combat with poles. The rivals face each other in the middle of an area of beaten earth, surrounded by an excited crowd. Both

contenders have a thin pole made of hard wood over 6.5 feet long and with the tip sculpted so as to symbolize a phallus. Often, strips of cotton are used to protect the combatants' heads and throat, while the back of the hands, the knees and elbows are covered with small baskets made of plant fiber. The purpose of the donga is not to kill or injure one's opponent, but to prove one's agility and dexterity. This does not mean that the combat entails no risks or shedding of blood; on the contrary, the wounds may be severe, but they are never mortal. Death, even if accidental, is punished with banishment from the village and confiscation of the guilty party's possessions. The contest, which involves dozens of combatants, is by elimination: the winner is carried in triumph to the edge of the arena, where he is greeted by a group of girls in festive dress, one of whom will choose him as her husband.

For the men, the heavy iron ornaments and large labret worn by their women are signs of elegance and prestige. The first European explorers were impressed and horrified by the deformations the Mursi women had to undergo. In order to make room for the heavy wooden or terracotta disc their lower incisors have to be removed, which is carried out with a rudimentary scalpel and is very painful. Furthermore, the excessive strain on the muscle tissue, which almost reaches the breaking point, creates difficulty in speaking and even in normal physiological functions such as eating and drinking. Bottego noted that the labret might be as much as over 3 inches in diameter; nowadays it is normally 7.8 inches, even though this custom is slowly declining. In reality, piercing one's lips to insert decorative objects is widespread in many areas of Africa, but only

The labret, which is typical decoration for both the Mursi and Surma, is considered a sign of beauty.

the Mursi and the Sara-Kobo in Chad have developed this custom to such a macroscopic degree. Once people thought that the labret, in deforming the face, acted as a deterrent against slave traders, since the human merchandise lost much of its value on the market. But if this were the case, why didn't the practice also involve men, who were sought after by the slave traders as free laborers? There is another fact that seems to invalidate the above theory. Such large-scale deformation of the lips takes a lot of time. The hole is enlarged gradually, with the progressive introduction of wooden cylinders of increasingly larger diameters, a process that takes years to finish. The totally isolated Mursi would therefore have had to foresee the arrival of the traders well beforehand, something that is obviously impossible and above all foreign to their fatalist mentality. The truth is probably much more simple. By generalizing, we can say that for many African populations the holes in the body are passages through which evil influences can enter and should therefore be defended. And there is no preventing the objects used for this purpose from becoming ornaments. Emulation, as well as the desire to distinguish oneself from others, may have led to a gradual increase in the size of the labret, which in a little more than a century reached its present dimensions. What in our opinion seems horrible and senseless is for the Mursi driven by pride and is a sign of beauty.

THE MURSI

A GUN AS A COMPANION

G ETTING TO THE LAND OF THE MURSI IS NO EASY UNDERTAKING. IT TAKES A COUPLE OF HOURS BY CAR FROM MAGO NATIONAL PARK, ALONG A TRACK THAT DISAPPEARS, ON IMPOSSI-BLE CLIMBS AND DESCENTS, WITH MUD AND ENORMOUS BOULDERS TO GET OVER AND IMPASS-ABLE VEGETATION WITH SHRUBS AND THORNS.

This stretch of road is the undisputed domain of the tsetse fly: the battle, which is waged inside a boil-ing hot vehicle with the doors and windows closed, is ferocious, with no holds barred. We usually win, but are exhausted afterwards. In the village the situation has not improved much. I think that this is the most aggressive tribe in the Omo River Valley: visitors are literally taken by storm. It's sheer hell. If you come here among the Mursi to work, you have to muster all your patience and a good dose of attention and pre-pare yourself to go through hours and hours of ten-sion. When you get out of your vehicle you are sur-rounded by brawny, nude six-foot tall men with prim-itive drawings on their bodies, women with labrets who always shout, and beautiful children who pounce on sweets and any sort of trinket or knick-knack.

The entire tribe touches you, pushes and pulls you, grabs your cameras. Unlike other ethnic groups, who ask for things, the Mursi expect them. Having emerged with difficulty from this inferno of the living, I ap-proach a boy with a sly smile. He asks me and asks me

again something that I do not understand and that sounds like this: "Uat is yo nem, ooair yu fum.... " I try to wriggle out of this conversation. The boy insists, laughs and tries again: "Uat is yo nem" and, pointing at himself, says: "Kwolilingo." "Ooair yu fum" and, point-ing at the ground with both hands: "Komba." "S Kom-ba beri gud" and, with a smile: "Ye, beri gud, deng yu." He repeats this four times, and at every "deng yu" he laughs more heartily. Finally the whole ritual of ques-tions and answers begins to make sense to me. In ex-temporaneous English, my interlocutor was asking me what my name was, where I was from, and whether I liked his village. I answer his questions and the con-versation ends with a "thank you" and a good laugh. I also laugh, because I thought he was asking me to give him something and because I didn't understand that he was only trying to communicate, either out of curiosi-ty or to show off the English he had learned God knows where and how. While the tribe in caught up in discussing with Zinabu – infinitely long haggling over the price of our tents, cars, and the guards, at the end of which everything begins all over again – Kwolilingo brings me a notebook. I open it and see drawings and reproductions of *bir*. He shows me the portrait of a li-on and in order to explain what it is he imitates its roar; he shows me a crocodile and points at the river; he draws my attention to the *bir* and counts with his fin-gers. And every so often he repeats it all over again,

On the road to Omomursi, three children scan the horizon from a solitary tree.

adding a comment that astounds me: "Komba, ye, beri gud. London, brr [and he hugs himself to mime cold weather]. Lalibela, brr [again mimicking cold]. Komba beri gud."   However, the Mursi are not all like Kwolilingo: they make it impossible for me to work and are always angry. On many occasions there is so much tension that the ranger who accompanies us has to raise his Kalashnikov to his shoulder. It's a tiring day and night. But I have my photos, and that's what counts.

When we get into the car to leave the village and go back on the tsetse-fly road, Kwolilingo shows me his notebook for the last time, repeats his "perform-

ance" in English and says goodbye with that strange "thank you" followed by a loud laugh.

I don't know if there's a school around here, of which Kwolilingo is probably the only student, but I like to think that if a school exists, in order to get there this Mursi, who is no longer a young boy, has to walk for hours on end and pass over hidden paths in the mountains, without clothes and shoes but with his notebook tucked under his arm. Maybe he sleeps in the open for days and then returns to his village, Komba, with one more drawing in his notebook and another word in English to use with the next tourist.

According to an ancient custom,
the domed huts of the Mursi
village of Komba lie together in a
clearing protected by a hedge.

The Mursi and the Omo River

A life on the shore

186

186-187 The life of the inhabitants of Omursi is confined to the village and the area as far as the bank of the Omo River.

188-189 and 190-191 At day's end, a group of men from Komba goes for a refreshing swim in the Mago River.

192-193 A Mursi warrior observes the situation in Komba from on high, while two women return to the village from the Mago River, where they went to get their daily supply of water.

194-195 A group of warriors armed with
Kalashnikovs on a huge tree at the edge
of the village of Komba.

196-197 In the village of Hailowa, two
Mursi girls are leading a cow after having
shaved artistic decorations on its hide
with a razor blade.

Mursi works

The granaries

These men at Komba
are building granaries.

The granaries are constructed by tying wooden
sticks together and then covering them with the
typical domes.

The cylindircal walls of the
granary are almost finished:
the men are about to build
the roof.

204 Everybody chips in to build the granaries: once the cylindrical foundation has been made, the men hoist it onto the supporting poles and then place the roof over it.

205 Lifting the "lid", women at work place sacks of grain in the granaries.

An unusual sight

The 'eye' of the stranger

The Mursi are very curious: this child can't resist
the temptation of looking through the camera.

All the villagers of Komba participate in the meeting held in the clearing in front of the huts while a man an armed man looks over the assembly.

The populace Assembled

In the ring to decide

The meetings are usually called by the village
chief to discuss problems or to provide
information and give instructions.

A WAR-LIKE NATURE
THE POLES OF COURAGE

A group of warriors in Komba improvises a Donga,
the traditional combat with poles.

Both Mursi men and women are at their ease with guns,
which are their constant companions.

READY FOR COMBAT

THE TREE OF GUNS

In Komba every man has his own Kalashnikov,
which he uses during hunts or in battles against
enemy ethnic groups.

Their face painting, guns
and fierce expression
add to the Mursi's
reputation of being
ferocious warriors.

221

Mursi men wear strange headdresses with
feathers and bright colors that are in striking
contrast with their harsh features.

The abstract patterns on the faces of the Mursi are quite elaborate and carefully executed

To underscore their proud character, the young Mursi paint themselves by putting their fingertips in a plaster paste.

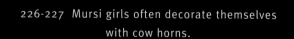

226-227 Mursi girls often decorate themselves
with cow horns.

228-229 Struck by the presence of foreigners,
a young girl from Komba smiles timidly at the
photographer.

A woman displays her strange "hairdo," which consists of cascades of metal curls instead

Besides horrns on their heads and white painting on their faces and bodies, the Mursi gir
wear gaudy iron ornaments in their lips.

ETHIOPIA 2003/04
"OMO VALLEY"

...THE HEAVY IRON
ORNAMENTS AND
LARGE LABRETS
WORN BY THEIR
WOMEN ARE SIGNS
OF ELEGANCE AND
PRESTIGE.

To make room for the labret, a painful operation is necessary: the lower incisors have to be removed with a scalpel or a chisel.

Another common decorative element used
by the Mursi women are shells gathered
from the river.

A man stares at the photographer's lens, his eyes manifesting all the pride of the Mursi

238-239 With ocher and plaster on his face,
a showy earring, and a feather hanging from
a braid, this boy reveals an aptitude for
aesthetic harmony.

240-241 The tradition of painting one's face
as a sign of beauty–as this woman has
done–or to intimidate one' enemies, is deep-
rooted in the Omo River Valley populations.

242-243 A little girl wearing gaudy and
heavy round iron earrings.

244-245 The fierce and aggressive Mursi
have been in conflict with their neighbors
for a long time, a state of belligerency
marked by raids, violence and abuse that
has left a deep scar in both the soul and
look of every man.

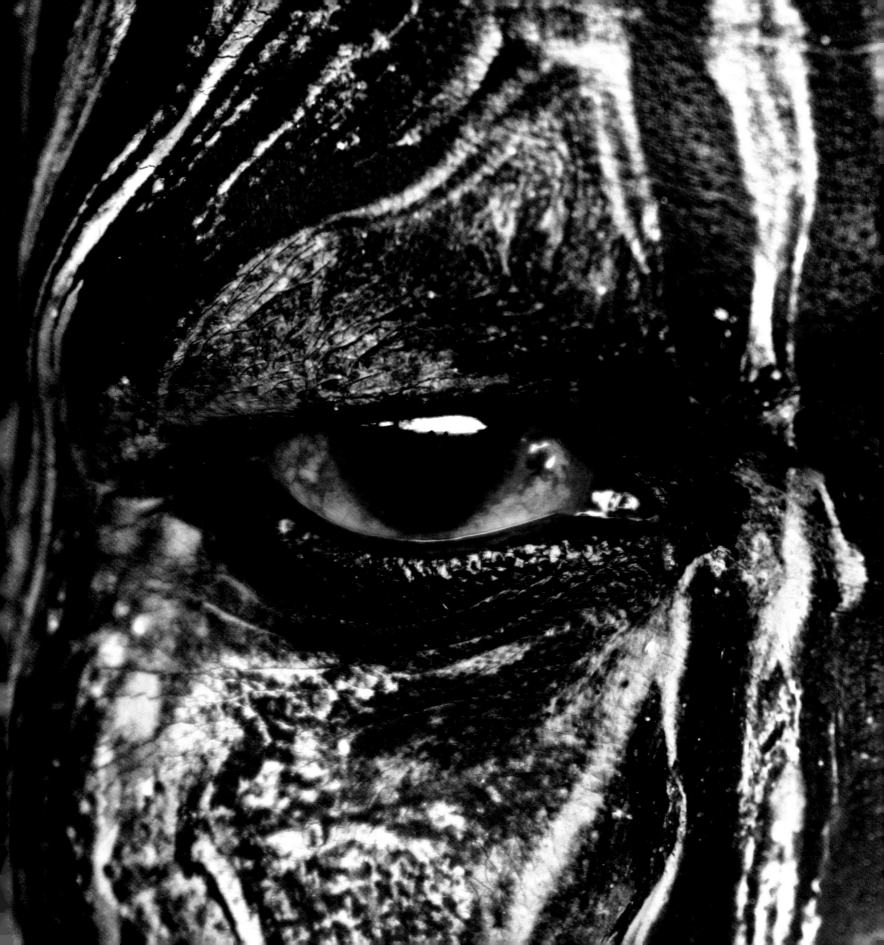

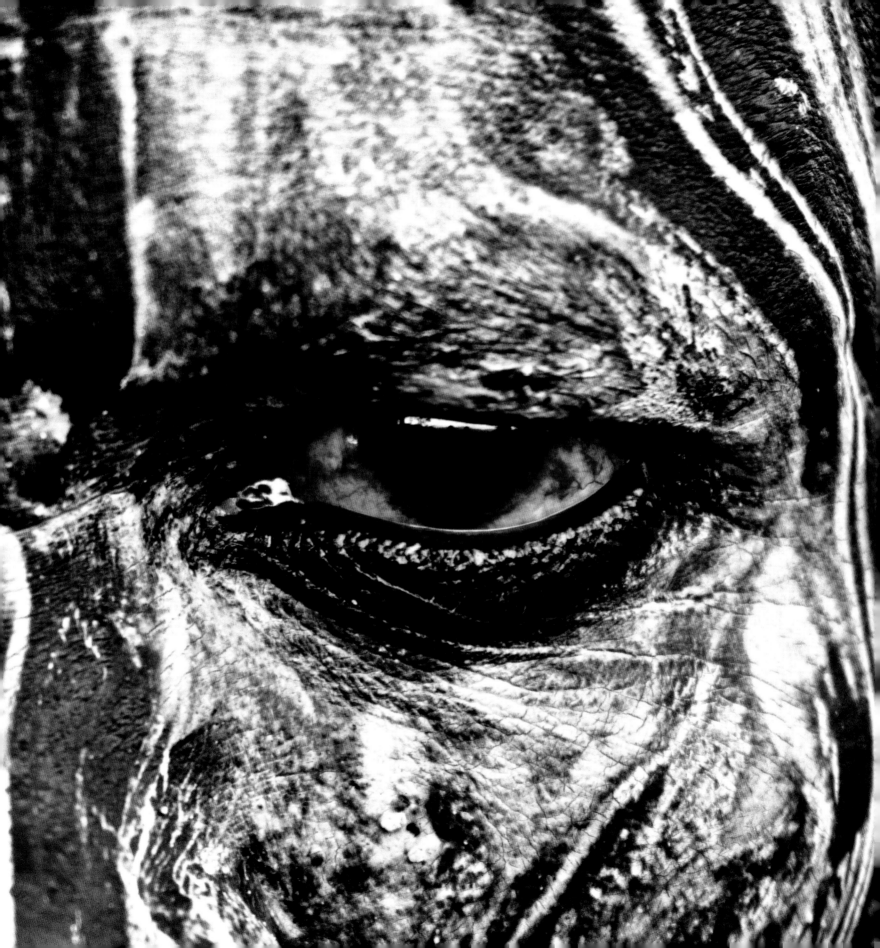

THE
BANNA

PROFESSIONALS
OF RITUAL

[PAOLO NOVARESIO]

THE BANNA

PROFESSIONALS OF RITUAL

T HE BANNA, OR BANYA, LIVE IN THE SURROUNDINGS OF THE MOUNTAINOUS REGION BETWEEN THE OMO AND WOITO RIVERS. THEIR LANGUAGE, WHICH IS VIRTUALLY THE SAME AS THE SPOKEN TONGUE OF THE HAMER AND BASHADA, IS OF OMOTIC ORIGIN.

These three ethnic groups have such close affinities that they could be considered a single entity, since their cultural heritage, political organization and strategies of economic survival are practically the same and the customs and rituals that mark their everyday life are similar, if not identical. On the other hand, their relationship with the Mursi and Bodi, their age-old enemies, is quite different, as it is characterized by a ruinous succession of wars and cattle raiding. The Banna are basically cow, sheep and goat herders. They also grow sorghum, sesame and corn, which they sow at the beginning of the rainy season. However, they tend to their fields quite unwillingly and often abandon them to their fate, so that the harvests are poor and certainly not enough to feed theirr families. Wild honey is their only surplus product: it is exchanged or sold in the markets along the road, thus affording the Banna enough money to be able to purchase indispensable goods and domestic utensils.

The chronic lack of foodstuffs is the reason for the marked mobility of this population. The transhumance routes they follow in search of new pastures are long and fatiguing and most of the Banna lead a semi-nomadic existence. The type of house they live in is a clear manifestation of this condition: their huts are mere shelters consisting of a framework of curved poles tied together and covered with grass or matting. In the middle of the village is the pen for the livestock, guarded by the men even at night. From a territorial standpoint Banna society is divided into two major sections, each of which is run by a *bitta* or ritual leader. According to oral tradition, the *bittas* and certain clans descend from an ancient stock of the Ari, their northern neighbors. As a result of this distant relationship, the ties between these two peoples are still quite close and friendly. In certain cases, those who boast a blood relationship with the Ari behave like a tribe within the tribe: they are required to follow the customs of their ancestors and not undergo circumcision, which is on the other hand obligatory for all the other youngsters.

The social organization of the Banna, albeit weak and foreign to rigid rules, is based on the age class system. The life of a man is marked by numerous passages, each of which represents a further step in respectability and power within the community. The top ring of this social ladder is occupied by the elders, who are endowed with special spiritual authority. Women, whether single or married, are relegated

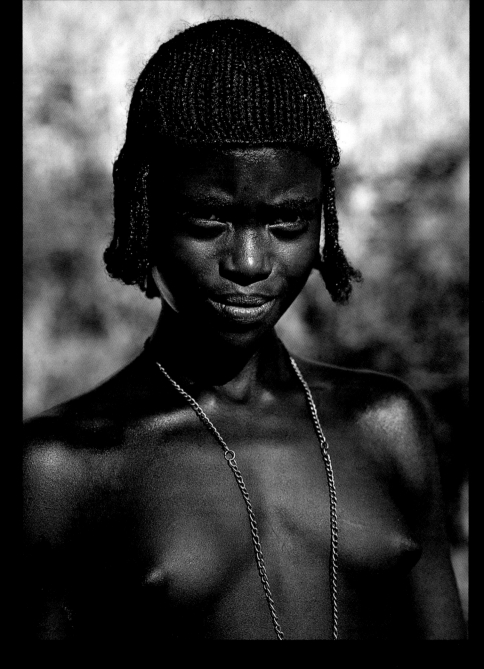

EBONY IN BRAIDS

The hairdo of braids and long iron necklace serve to highlight the naive charm of this girl

to a subordinate position. There is no particular rite after adolescence that marks the attainment of full womanhood, whereas for the males the transition from childhood to the first stage of adulthood is a moment of crucial importance. The Banna, like the Hamer, Bashada and other populations in this area, celebrate this event with a series of initiation rites that culminate in the" Bull's Leap." Only after this final public manifestation of courage and skill is the youth considered a full-fledged man who can marry. The preparation for the "Bull's Leap" is long and elaborate. The *maz*, the young men who have already gone through initiation, see to the various phases of this rite. Their bodies covered with butter and their faces painted with lime and ocher, they gather to sip an infusion of coffee, a consecrated beverage. This collective libation is the prelude to the true ceremony. As if in a collective frenzy, the *maz* repeatedly strike the young female relatives of the future initiate with long, supple batons. This is by no means "make-believe"; on the contrary, the flogging is heavy and causes bloody wounds. And yet the women accept this punishment stoically, even begging to be flogged, since tolerating pain is a demonstration of love for and devotion to their relative.

But the most difficult task for the *maz* is to set up the arena for the leap. In the middle of a flat excavated area they place about thirty cows packed closely together side by side. In the meantime, the boy about to be initiated is solemnly given the *boko*, a short cane in the shape of a phallus which, when inserted in the circle made by a row of iron armbands to simulate the sexual act, symbolizes the birth and beginning of a new life. The youth is comforted by his companions and is purified, so that he is now ready to face the supreme test: he must leap onto the back of the first cow and run over this precarious "walkway" to the end, trying to keep his balance and not fall. This test is repeated four times in a row, forward and backward. One fall, though considered a bad omen, does not entail any particular punishment and is usually attributed to external causes such as a sudden gust of wind or an unexpected movement on the part of the animals. But should the boy fall a second time the consequences are irreparable: for his entire life he will be the object of severe social sanctions, and will be mocked and despised by all the members of the village for his failure.

Succeeding in executing the "Bull's Leap" correctly means entry into a new world, a sort of interregnum between childhood and adulthood: the status of the *maz* is enveloped in an aura of purity and harmony. The youths wander from one house to another and receive gifts and offerings of honey, coffee and meat, for which they will give thanks later with songs. During moonlit nights, the sounds of the lyre flutter through the silent village. This ancient instrument passes from one person to another, accompanying a moving and plaintive litany that seems to come from the hereafter.

A boy with his Kalashnikov, is wearing a gaudy colored fabric; on his head
is a strip of glass beads, similar to the earring in both motifs and color.

THE BANNA

DANCING THE IWAGANDI

"THE BARS ARE NEXT TO THE BROTHELS, AND THEY REGURGITATE MUSIC FULL BLAST AND COFFEE FOR TRUCK DRIVERS," SAYS THE LONELY PLANET GUIDE UNDER THE HEADWORD "SHASHEMENE."

We are in the Rift Valley, heading south on the Transafrican, the large road that cuts Africa in half and connects Cairo with Capetown.

The day is cool and clear, and finding ourselves at a temperature of 20° C at only a short distance from the Equator, is really surprising (it is 37° at Rome). Traveling among goats and cows we pass by the Zuqala volcano and, farther along, Mt. Meki, followed by Lake Langano and Lake Shala; at the Shashemene junction, the last outpost of perdition, we leave the Transafrican and head toward Sodo. After going through large banana plantations, we arrive at Arba Minch, the city of the 40 springs, just in time to see, from the splendid panoramic terrace of the Bekele Mola Hotel, the umpteenth cloudburst pouring down in front of us on Lake Abajo and Lake Chamo.

At Arba Minch the paved road comes to an end and the dirt road begins, full of dust and pitfalls. And no sooner do we set off at dawn than we meet the first obstacle, which looks like an innocuous puddle. When Paolo comes to the enormous marsh, despite the fact that he spots cars and trucks mo-tionless on the other side, he suspects nothing and decides to try to pass through. We get stuck on the first attempt; one, two, three maneuvers to get out come to nothing: the more we insist, the more we get bogged down in the mud. A few minutes later the water begins to filter through the door and floods the inside of our Toyota, which is leaning precariously at a 30° angle on a rise. We risk overturning the vehicle and seriously jeopardizing our journey, which has just begun. Zinabu arrives, amid the din of shouts and laughter of a group of children. We don't know whether they are trying to give us a hand or whether they intend to make our discomfort last as long as possible into order to earn more *bir* for the "disinterested" help they offer us. There are about twenty of them, and they all begin pushing us, with the water up to their waists, in order to get the car out of the mud. After a half-hour of vain struggling, a tractor arrives opportunely from God knows where, a steel cable is fastened to the Toyota, and in a second it pulls us out of that difficult position. The children, all spattered with mud, receive payment for their help, this time in silence: 2 *bir* each. And we can finally continue our journey.

We pass the river on a level with the Gidole market to arrive at the more colorful one at Konso. We cross the huge terracing typical of this region and begin to descend toward the Weyto Valley. For to-

A flood scene: with the help of the natives, the off-roaders manage to free themselves from the quagmire.

day our trip ends near the Banna village of Hallatori, and under a full moon we spend our first night camping to the sound of the songs of a nearby tribe.

Dawn. A light rain. Outside the tent some boys are waiting for something, perhaps to see what we look like, since we arrived in the evening and they didn't get a good look at us. Anaylem lights the fire and makes coffee while Paolo and Zinabu speak with a Banna, who has come see us at our camp in order to organize a visit at his village not far away.

After a short walk over a hill we arrive in a village with no more than 30 persons. This is my first meeting with the valley people: the Banna show a great sense of hospitality and a predisposition to kindness. Elegant in their ways, with kind looks, they live in rather large huts. Leaning against their houses in full view are all the tools they need for their work in the fields. Each hut has its own enclosure and, around it, the cornfield, which in this season is luxuriant.

All of a sudden the youngsters begin to dance in our honor: it is the iwagandi, a ritual symbolizing a man courting a woman. The girls in the middle jump while approaching the boys who, in turn, following the companion they have chosen, mime a gesture much like the sexual act. The dance ritual lasts for several hours and almost always ends with copulation. During the dance, the man who has hosted us follows our every move with apprehension: he is worried about a delicate little plant that may be trampled on by all these people moving in the enclosure of his hut. Several times during the dance I see him protect the area, but a moment of distraction and the plant is crushed underfoot and falls to the ground. The man picks it up delicately and tries to straighten it, but in vain: it simply will not stand up. He tries again, but the little plant falls once more. He insists, setting a small stick next to it to support it: a tiny gesture that is an act of love, just like the one that in a short time will take place between the two young Banna as a tribute to life.

THE IWAGANDI
DANCING COURTSHIP

The Iwagandi—or Dance of Night—is a courtship
ritual that involves all the village youth.

The Banna are not at all belligerent; on the contrary,
they are quite hospitable and here demonstrate their
expansiveness by improvising the Iwagandi.

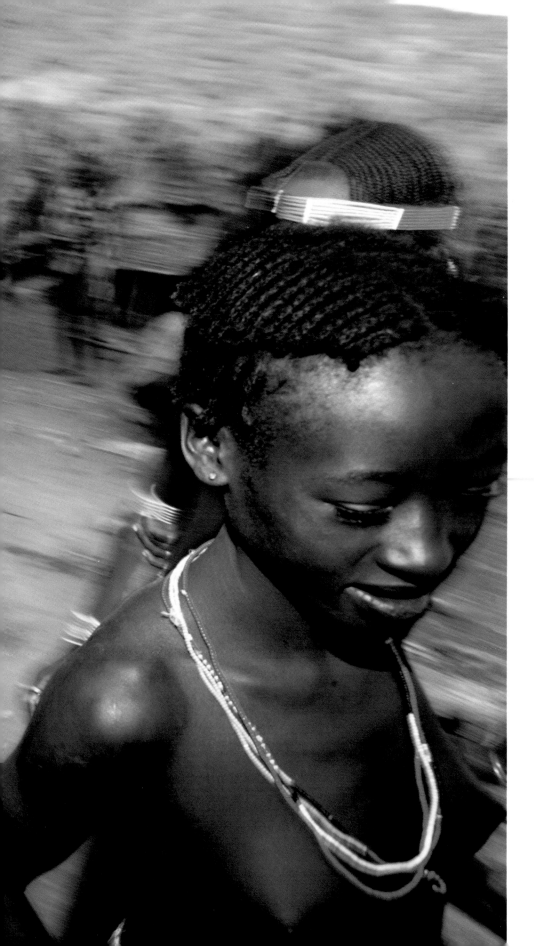

From 258 to 261
The courtship begins: the dancing
women approach the partner they have
chosen, who also demonstrates his
interest by dancing. The dance lasts to
the wee hours and usually culminates
in coitus.

THE
ERBORE

IN THE LAND
OF SALT

[PAOLO NOVARESIO]

THE ERBORE

IN THE LAND OF SALT

THE REGION SURROUNDING CHEW BAHIR LAKE IS BASICALLY FLAT AND ARID. THE ERBORE VILLAGE IS THE LAST SOUTHERN OUTPOST IN ETHIOPIA. BEYOND IT, TOWARD THE BORDER WITH KENYA, THE ROAD BECOMES A NETWORK OF DUSTY TRACKS THAT SEEM TO VANISH INTO THIN AIR.

The sky and earth merge in a horizon that is vague and bewildering due to mirages and often becomes dark because of sudden dust storms. A sterile stretch of mud, along with a few wells containing murky water, is all that remains of Lake Stefanie, which was discovered by Teleki a little more than a century ago. It has been decades since the waters of the Woito, the sole confluent of the lake, have reached the middle of this basin, which has run dry. Yet in this land without hope, the seasonal flooding of the river miraculously creates a kind of linear oasis, a thin strip of fertile land wrested from the arid desert on which the Erbore people cultivate sorghum and corn, which are essential for their survival. The banks of the Woito are periodically regenerated by the silt and provide pasture for the livestock, which is the second basic element of the local economy. Although they depend on agricultural products for their subsistence, the Erbore regard them-

selves as pastoralists: cows, goats and sheep are the basic standards of value for all their economic transactions, they are the assets needed to marry, and they play an important role in rituals. The Erbore, also known as Hor, number about 6,500, divided in large groups. The Marle, considered the original, pure stock, live along the banks of Chew Bahir Lake. Recently, after a long period of conflict with the Hamer, most of the Marle moved west of the Woito River, where the Borana offered them hospitality. The Gandarobba, on the other hand, are the group with the most power and prestige and occupy the more northerly territory, around the Erbore town. Indeed, the present-day Erbore are the result of the aggregate of various ethnic groups that with time merged and became a single people.

Mixed marriages with girls from other tribes are the rule to this day: a man can look for a wife among the Borana, the Dhaasanac, the Rendille or any other group, except for the Hamer, their enemies. However, marriages with Tsamai women, who are not circumcised, are disapproved. For even more unfathomable reasons, the Konso women are also regarded unfavorably, even though many Erbore use the Konso language as a *lingua franca*. Borana is spoken by everyone, and certain lower caste fractions such as the Waata Won-

This girl's intense expression is softened by the large colored chokers and by her instinctive "coquetry" when exhibiting her spiral iron earrings.

Erbore women pay particular attention to their dress.

do use it as an everyday language. The very term "Erbore" stems from Borana.

Oral tradition ascribes the origin of the Erbore to two mythical ancestors sent by the god Waq to build the first villages on the two shores of the river. But most Erbore now say they descend from ancient Borana stock, as can be seen by the terminology used to indicate numerous clans. This controlled strategy of assimilation and exclusion has allowed the Erbore to preserve their distinct personality and defend their customs while continuing to maintain fruitful contact with the outside world.

First-rate mediators, the Erbore enjoyed a certain amount of prosperity in the past. The European explorers who visited the Woito delta at the end of the 19th century were struck by their wealth: wearing elegant clothes from the coast of Somalia and adorned with

brass and ivory bracelets, the Erbore had thousands of head of livestock and abundant supplies of sorghum. Bottego described them in September 1896 as merchants and polyglots who were extremely skillful in maintaining the monopoly of all the trade in the region: "This small population is well known even in distant lands precisely because of its commercial activity; this importance stems from the neutrality that allows the Erbore to go anywhere. They stop the Safara, who are Somali traders, from going west of the lake because they themselves want to buy ivory from the Galeb, the Karo and Mursi and then sell it again for a huge profit. They are quite hospitable with the caravans, provided they can maintain the above prerogative, which makes them famous in the field of ivory trade."

The social organization of the Erbore is based on the

Erbore men wear colored fabrics on their heads that often have printed floral motifs.

system of age groups. The different generations, which in turn are divided into four classes, succeed to power about every forty years, after a long and elaborate series of ceremonies. The duty of the political leaders is to dispense justice, manage the relations with the bordering populations, and regulate the ownership of the land and animals. The fields are distributed on a seasonal basis to the various families, which must respect the rules handed down by tradition. Those guilty of negligence in work may be excluded from the distribution of land and condemned to harsh punishment, including whipping. Harvest surplus is used to purchase salt, coffee and everyday items. The Konso and Hamer artisans provide iron tools, earthenware vases and other articles that the Erbore are not able to produce on their own. Besides meeting economic needs, this system of intertribal exchanges guarantees peace and security in the area, making war a disadvantageous affair for everyone concerned. The authority wielded by the generation groups is balanced by that of the religious chiefs, the so-called *kawot*, whose position is hereditary. They play an essentially spiritual role, as they are asked to pray for the well-being of the society and ensure success in battle or during raids. Only the *kawot* can carry out sacrifices and ask God for rain. The very fertility of the Earth depends on their benedictions and ability in managing relations with the supernatural world. Every year the *kawot* "fatten" the waters of the Woito by burying a sheep's tail in the dry riverbed. Thanks to this offering, the precious silt will continue to be deposited on the fields and the sorghum will thrive. And the Erbore will continue to live in keeping with the traditions of their fathers, viewing themselves as unique.

[GIANNI GIANSANTI]

TRAVEL NOTES

T HE ERBORE LIVE BETWEEN THE SA-VANNA AND THE MOUNTAINS IN LARGE REED HUTS THAT FROM A DISTANCE LOOK LIKE OVERTURNED PIROGUES.

They are very poor but they have a sort of dignified fascination about them that is particularly evident in the women. I knew that the Erbore women wear only a heavy animal skin skirt, have long, thin braids and love to adorn themselves with pearls. But many of them have shaven heads and some even wear a long black veil – which they grip tightly in their hands – that leaves only the face exposed. The first image I recall upon my arrival in the village concerns three little girls: they were dressed in this kind of chador, gave me a timid glance and, after letting themselves be photographed, ran away in fear from my lens.

The men proudly display brightly colored T-shirts and a sort of wraparound loincloth. Some also wear trousers. But what strikes you is the amount of jewelry every woman wears on her body: chokers, ornaments, bracelets and, above all, huge iron anklets. Consequently, every step a woman takes is accompanied by the tinkling and jingling of metal.... But even as prisoners of these cumbersome jewels and with their heads shaven, the Erbore women are beautiful.

Africa has always been a source of inspiration for artists because of its light, scents, sounds and people. People go to the Black Continent in search of new faces and bodies for the high fashion catwalks or for entertainment spectacles: women who have retained the uncontaminated spirit of their land in their look and movements. I once found inspiration and beauty in a statuesque and solitary girl standing erectly in the middle of green shrubbery and watching us from far off. Her hair braided, beads of sweat on her black forehead, her bare breasts barely visible under a mountain of necklaces, tight bracelets on her forearms that defy her blood circulation: I must have photographed her at least a hundred times to try to capture the beauty she emanated, the bitter expression, the wild look.

For more than ten minutes, when I was taking my shots, she remained virtually immobile with a model's pose, her hands resting on her hips, her neck outstretched, looking far off in the savanna.

And I must confess that I was completely disappointed when she decided that we had worked enough and that it was now time for her to be paid. For that matter, models are paid for their services all over the world....

269 Often wrapped in long veils, Erbore women seem to take on the mysterious appearance typical of Muslim women.

270-271 Like a black Venus, a beautiful girl stops in the clearing in front of the village, amused at the idea of having her picture taken.

272-273 The Erbore village lies in the middle of a luxuriant valley surrounded by mountains. Its tall huts are made of reeds and various kinds of planks.

274 The Erbore

Just outside the village,
two children play at being
guards on a shelter above
a sorghum field.

THE ERBORE WOMEN

FASCINATION AND MYSTERY

Adolescent Erbore girls usually cut off their
hair and decorate their heads with narrow
bands of colored glass beads.

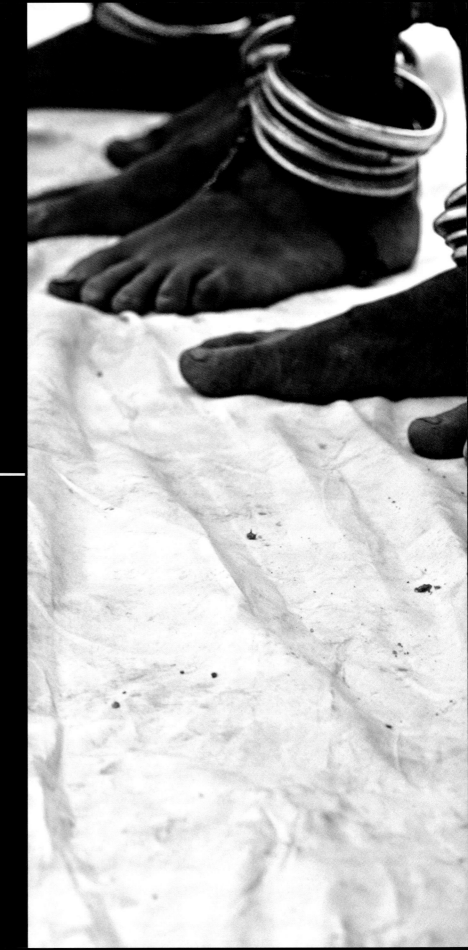

ANKLETS

THE CLANGOR OF IRON

Traditionally the Erbore use iron as a
decorative element. The women in
particular wear huge and heavy anklets,
and their movements are always
accompanied by the clangor of the metal.

...EVEN LIKE THIS, PRISONERS OF THOSE CUMBERSOME JEWELS AND WITH THEIR HEADS SHAVED, THE ERBORE WOMEN ARE STRIKINGLY BEAUTIFUL.

With her intense look, full lips, spiral rings and necklaces, this young girl epitomizes the Erbore ideal of beauty.

A splendid girl displays her colored ornaments and metal jewels

THE PEACEFUL FACE OF THE OMO RIVER

THE KONSO

THE ARTISANS OF ETHIOPIA

[PAOLO NOVARESIO]

THE KONSO

THE ARTISANS OF ETHIOPIA

A FEW DOZEN MILES SOUTH OF LAKE CHAMO, THE EAST SPURS OF THE RIFT VALLEY FADE AWAY IN A VAST MOUNTAINOUS REGION THAT FACES THE SAVANNAS AND DESERTS IN THE BORDERLAND BETWEEN KENYA AND ETHIOPIA.

This territory, bounded by the broad curve formed by the Sagan River, is the home of the Konso, who number about 185,000. Of Borana origin, the name Konso really indicates three different groups that basically share the same language, culture, and economic system.

The history of the Konso and Borana is closely linked. For centuries both populations have been living in a sort of symbiosis that goes well beyond mere trade exchanges. Like their neighbors, the Konso base their social organization on age classes, membership in which is much more important than lineage. The rites and ceremonies that mark the transition from one level to a superior one – in keeping with a fixed calendar that covers the entire lifetime of the person – are extraordinarily alike. Both the Konso and the Borana wear on their foreheads a *kalacha*, an ornament in the shape of a phallus and a sign of prestige that among other things has the power to preserve virility.

The Konso craftsmen, famous for their manual dexterity, provide the nomadic Borana with the precious products of sedentary civilization: cotton cloth, tools, wooden bowls, and a wide range of luxury items. Weaving and metalworking are activities reserved for the men, while the women are responsible for tanning and pottery. In the markets, which are held every day in a different locality, there is an abundance of farm produce: coffee, cereals and legumes are exchanged for bars of salt and animals for slaughter.

The Konso are diligent and unflagging farmers, able to obtain the maximum from a plot of poor land. A constant problem they have to face is that the rain causes erosion in the steep slopes of the hills and impoverishes the soil by washing it away. Therefore they terrace their farmland, which is shored up by long dry-stone walls; the cultivated area covers a surface area of over 250 square miles, that is tilled with the help of a two-pronged hoe and systematically fertilized with dung and other organic matter.

Standing out in this geometric, markedly humanized landscape are the *waka*, anthropomorphic stelae erected to commemorate important persons and heroes of the past. Around

287 The Konso market is the most lively and colorful in the entire Omo Valley, into the mountainous heart of Ethiopia.

290-291 A boy poling his precarious craft through the waters of crocodile-infested Lake Chamo.

each figure, portrayed with stylized features, are the images of the enemies he killed, as well as the women and other persons dear to him.

Protected by the hieratic glance of the *waka* and thanks to incessant labor, the Konso farmers can count on two good harvests a year that correspond to the two rainy seasons, which occur in spring and autumn. They plant wheat and barley on the slopes, while sorghum for the most part is planted at lower altitudes. Indeed, the Konso have no fewer than 24 varieties of this latter, each one with its own specific characteristics. Besides the above products, the Konso also grow cotton, tobacco, tubers and vegetables. An important source of food are the edible leaves of certain species of tall trees such as *Moringa stenopetala*, which is known throughout East Africa for its nutritional and disinfectant qualities.

The Konso also gather wild honey and breed cattle, goats and sheep, whose milk is used mainly for the smaller children or to make butter. The animals are rarely slaughtered, only on occasion of ceremonies or particularly important social events. Hunting and the gathering of wild fruit are rare activities: all birds, eggs, fish and most wild fauna are in fact protected by taboos.

In the turbulent ethnic mosaic of southern Ethiopia the Konso are an exception: although they esteem courage and virility, they are generally foreign to all forms of violence. Murder is severely punished and conflicts are avoided as much as possible. Certain types of weapons such as spears with beak-shaped tips, which can inflict severe wounds, are prohibited by Konso custom: shedding blood offends Waq and contaminates the purity of Mother Earth, whose gifts are indispensable for the material subsistence of society. Meek and peaceful by nature, the Konso have elaborated special rites of reconciliation that are carried out both in case of war and intestine disputes.

The administration of justice is entrusted to the elders, who meet in council. Those guilty of a crime, the object of public scorn, risk being banished from the village or deprived of the community's support in case of need. The Konso have a strong sense of solidarity. Collective mutual aid is needed to build terraces, excavate wells, and irrigate the crops during droughts and to cope with natural calamities. Another result of cooperation are the tall stone walls that surround the villages, which are usually placed in an elevated position in order to be easily defended.

A network of paths marked off by wooden

fences connects the various parts of the village, which is divided into quarters. Stone and wood are not only the basic elements of the solid and long-lasting Konso architecture, but are also used daily. The former serves to mill the cereals, as the inner dressing of the wells, and to sharpen farm tools and weapons.

Inside these fortified quarters each family has its own private space, which is also fenced, inside of which are the granary, the animal enclosures and several round thatch-roofed huts for the head of the family, the first-born son, the oldest wife, and the various children. After marrying, the youngest sons are encouraged to find a new house as soon as possible.

Public areas used for meetings and ceremonies are in all the districts. A superficial observer might regard the Konso villages as senseless labyrinths arranged chaotically. But in reality their obsessive parceling expresses an analytic and meticulous mentality, the habit of exploiting every possible piece of land in a harsh and often hostile environment. Rainfall may be too heavy and cause ruinous floods, or it may be totally lacking and parch the soil in depth. And if drought persists, the efficient farming techniques and capacities accumulated over the centuries are meaningless, because nothing can be done to stem famine, hunger and malnutrition. The harmony of the universe, the fruit of human labor and divine benevolence, is continuously threatened by disorder. Beyond the checkerboard of the cultivated fields lies a mysterious world, the domain of demons and spirits that are active mostly at night. These malign creatures live in trees, in the bottom of wells, and wander ceaselessly along the borders of the villages. If they are evoked or disturbed they may provoke madness, sterility, illness and death. At times they possess human beings and use them to their own ends. Even dreams are endangered: the ghosts of the dead sometimes visit the living by entering their dreams, which is considered an ill omen. In order to cope with this host of supernatural beings the Konso make use of clairvoyants, who are the only persons who can reveal the source of evil and, with the aid of magic, free the victim from the nefarious influences that have struck him or her.

Although it is hard and fraught with problems, the life of the Konso also has many pleasant aspects. Music and dance are common forms of entertainment, especially at sunset, when the torrid heat of midday is transformed into balmy evening. Then Waq, the benevolent Lord of the Sky, seems to return to live together with humans, as it was in the beginning.

[GIANNI GIANSANTI]

THE KONSO

PARADISE REGAINED

D URING MY TRIPS IN ETHIOPIA I HAVE OFTEN CROSSED OVER THE KONSO AREA, THE LAST FRONTIER BEFORE DESCENDING INTO THE EASTERN REGIONS OF THE OMO RIVER VALLEY.

This is a true border region; beyond it, there is no trace of what we commonly refer to as civilization. The first time we stopped here we had just finished two weeks in the low valley among the Benna, Mursi, Hamer and Galeb, around the Mago National Park.

We arrived in the village of Goeha, where we set up camp toward evening, when the air becomes cool and the colors are bright. The village's central clearing and the panorama surrounding it were quite different from the Africa we had visited up to then. The field, whose grass was cut like that of a golf course, was bounded by low stone walls, in the construction of which the Konso are experts, since they had to learn to cultivate land consisting of soft hills and terraced gardens. No one was waiting to greet us except an old man who spoke to himself and told us of what he

remembered of "Little Black Face." He was considered the "village idiot." We came to Konso after days and days of the savanna, lakes populated by crocodiles and hippopotami and rowdy tribes, and we were amazed to find ourselves in a sort of Ethiopian Switzerland.

During our stay we met only a couple of persons besides the confused old man, who spent all his time playing *gabata*.

Zinabu explained the reason for the unusual calm and tranquility in the village: the king of Konso, Welde Dawit Keyote, who lived right where we had set up camp, was very ill and out of respect the inhabitants were careful not to make any noise. We also observed silence, finally appreciating its virtues once again.

I return to Konso four months later, again after weeks of intense work in the area of the Hamer and Mursi, and once more I experience the same sensation of peace, relief and freshness while admiring the gardens, small tree-lined streets, and woods. The silence, consisting of the leaves stirring in the wind and birdsong, reminds me of a story that I read some-

The huts in the Konso villages, surrounded by enclosures for the goats and fowl, have conical roofs made of reeds that are crowned by large terracotta vases used to secure the former.

where about the spirits of a place that were able to proliferate only where Man's presence had not been felt, and this leads me to meditate on the fascination the apparent immobility of these places has for visitors, immersed in a Nature that has prevailed over Man. Zinabu arrives and interrupts my thoughts to ask me if I might be interested in taking a photograph of a dead man. After my amazement at this question, he explains that the king died last June, a few days after our departure, and that it was the custom among the Konso people to keep the remains in a hut where they would be mummified and then buried only nine years, nine months and nine days after his death. After his physical death, to be precise, because according to the Konso, until the burial the deceased is really only very ill. This is the reason why the body is constantly under surveillance in the hut, where some guardians attend to it with the utmost solicitude: they bathe it three times a day, change the clothes, and stay next to it all the time, without ever sleeping.

I go to photograph the corpse, while Zinabu provides me with information about the local culture. The Konso are basically animists and believe everything around them has an occult power; they therefore worship the *waka*, funerary statues made in honor of chiefs or warriors who have demonstrated special courage that are placed next to the fields or on the main roads so that they can watch over the traffic of the passers-by, the world of the living.

This is the tradition. But, as we know, traditions and customs change according to necessity, and so I am told that the body of the king will be buried soon because there isn't enough money to feed the guardians. By the same token, the *waka* statues, which are very much sought after by collectors and enemies alike, are now kept together in the same hut so that there is only one guard to pay for.

I go into the hut. The king, or what is left of him, is there, fully dressed, bending over a stool, and in a state of decomposition. I notice that his face has been meticulously reconstructed. The effect is striking: there is something tragically comic about the work done to him and about the frightened glance of a guard, who is terrified by the smell. However, I think of the story of the spirit of place and the animist religion and of the fact that what I see before me was once a man, or rather a king....

I'm not the kind of person who believes in presences, spirits or souls the live after death. And I don't believe in it even when I grab my video camera to take a shot and there appears on the display a skull indicating an error with a word in red: ATTENTION...

295 top The mummified corpse of Welde Davit Keyote, the Konso king who died in June, is protected by a guardian. According to Konso tradition, his body should be preserved for nine years, nine months, nine weeks and nine days before being buried.

295 bottom Waka are wooden statues sculpted as a tribute to valorous chiefs and warriors, whose spirit they preserve.

Tamed land

Huts and terraces

The Konso villages, which lie on
verdant hills, are distinguished by their
terraced gardens, which are laid out by
the expert hands of this ethnic group.

A ROYAL VILLAGE

THE SOVEREIGN'S RESIDENCE

298

298-299 In the village of the king of the
Konso, two men play *gabata*, a typical
pastime in this region of Ethiopia.

300-301 A group of Konso youths return to
the village with heavy faggots of
wood on their backs.

Young Konso
The fatigue of living

302-303 Fatigued by her heavy load,
a girl stops to rest on the road
leading to the market.

304-305 From their early childhood
on, the young Konso women are
used to carry the heaviest loads.

...THE KONSO ARE DILIGENT AND UNFLAGGING FARMERS, ABLE TO OBTAIN THE MAXIMUM FROM A POOR PLOT OF LAND.

307 Konso women wear a traditional flounce skirt that always has the colors of the Ethiopian flag.

308-309 Large bundles of vegetables are ready to be sold or traded at the Konso market.

THE SINGING WATER

THE
BORANA

THE CHILDREN
OF DAWN

[PAOLO NOVARESIO]

THE BORANA

THE CHILDREN OF DAWN

THE WATER COMES UP SLOWLY FROM THE DEPTHS OF THE EARTH, TO THE RHYTHM OF AN OBSESSIVE SINGSONG. THE MASTER SINGER, VARYING THE TONES AND INTENSITY OF HIS VOICE, ESTABLISHES THE RHYTHM OF THE LABOR AND THE ANIMALS' ACCESS TO THE WATERING PLACES SO THAT NOT EVEN ONE DROP OF WATER IS WASTED.

These are the "Singing Wells" of the Borana people, a marvel of logistical and poetic organization. All around, as far as the eye can see, there is nothing else but low hills blackened by the sun and parched plains. The soil is covered with thorny scrub sometimes interrupted by patches of dry grass ruffled by the merciless wind. The countryside around Dublock, halfway between the village of Yabello and the Kenya border, seems to negate all hope of men and animals being able to survive there. Dublock is one of the most important watering spots in the region, one of the very few that can be used even during the long dry season. There are about twenty wells and no one is able to say with any degree of precision how and when they were excavated by cutting through the rock for dozens of feet with a technology that one imagines must have been primitive: a tremendous task and achievement, certainly the fruit of a rich society with noteworthy organizational means and ability. A series of tall stone steps leads to the bottom of the hole, to the spring. Bringing up water is a complicating and fatiguing job that involves dozens of men. For the Borana herders it is a necessity if they want to survive with their herds. The Borana are part of the large Oromo ethnic group, of which they regard themselves as the original and purest members, the only ones who have handed down the glorious traditions of their ancestors. In fact, they call themselves "The Children of Dawn," the favorites of Waq, the supreme god. The land of the Borana extends from the basin of the Juba River to the shores of Lake Chew Bahir and the hills inhabited by the Konso, and takes in vast regions of northern Kenya as well. This immense territory, which is for the most part flat desert, has a yearly rainfall of no more than 12 inches, concentrated in the months of November and December. Because of the torrid heat during the day and the lack of clouds, the area is practically lacking in surface water. In such an environment, nomadic life is an imperative. Consequently, the existence of the Borana depends on their livestock, their main source of food and sole possession.

This group of Borana is caught up in the difficult task of drawing water from the 'singing wells.'

Goats and sheep provide meat and milk in abundance, while the donkeys and camels are used above all as pack animals and merchandise for trade. But it is the cattle that are the tangible sign of a man's wealth and social status.

The Borana are deeply in love with their animals. For them cows are everything: a cultural benchmark, the symbol of power, and the object of complex rituals. This animal is the protagonist of religious sacrifices and is used as currency in payment of the bride price. Furthermore, these animals are used as compensation for an offence; depending on the seriousness of the crime committed, the guilty party has to pay the victim a certain number of cows. Sanctions may be quite severe: insulting someone may cost an ox, rustling cattle from a fellow member of the tribe is punished with a fine equal to five times the number of cattle stolen, whereas damages for murder consist of the payment of 100 head of cattle. The humpbacked zebu of East Africa certainly merits such high esteem since it is an extremely hardy species that resists disease and is able to withstand the continuous, long migrations in the desert in search of new pastureland. The Boranas' house is perfectly suited for nomadic life: it is made up of a framework of curved branches covered with interwoven palm leaves and can be taken down quickly and easily transported on camelback to the next destination. Setting up the camp, like all manual labor, is considered too undignified a job for a man and this

work is therefore done by the women, who in a few hours are able to "create" a village proper in the middle of nowhere. The women are also expected to draw the water, gather the firewood, milk the animals and, naturally, take care of the children. The men carry out more noble tasks such as excavating the wells and watering the animals. In certain periods of the year the Borana concentrate on extracting salt, which is found at the bottom of some volcanic craters. The small El Sod Lake, not far from the Dublock wells, is the most famous of these sources of salt; its black water conceals large saline deposits that the herders have exploited since ancient times. In fact, this lake provides different types of salt: the white variety, whose quality varies according to the depth of the deposit, is used by the Borana, while the mineral-rich dark mud that covers the bottom of the lake is for the animals. Salt is also a commodity in trade, a collateral activity of the tribe during their long trips in which meat, animal products and sometimes ivory are exchanged for cereals, tea, tobacco and honey, especially with the Konso farmers.

But the main activity of the Borana males is defending the group from possible attacks on the part of hostile tribes. For this people war is an inevitable necessity. Stability and harmony are extremely important values among the Borana but they lose all meaning with reference to the neighboring populations, who by definition are enemies and rivals in the division of the natural resources of this region. The aggressive behavior towards foreigners and outsiders is considered a virtue, and taking possession of their goods is a right. Whoever kills an enemy can wear a heavy ivory armband as a trophy that proves his valor. Bravery in battle is an indispensable quality for those who want to be considered *diira*, that is, virile. The Boranas' military epic is a celebration of carnage: their songs and legends honor mythical personages, great warriors whose exploits are set as examples for the youth. Madd Boru Dada is one of the most famous Borana heroes; an invincible fighter who also plundered huge multitudes of animals, he is known for the campaign he led in the mid-1800s against the Arsi, when he almost succeeded in wiping them off the face of the earth. The poor Arsi, who are distant cousins of the Borana, were responsible for having treacherously assassinated one of Dada's best friends.

The Boranas' weapons are simple but efficient: a heavy spear for hand-to-hand combat, a javelin, shield and sword. Firearms have partly modified combat techniques, but not the war philosophy of the Borana. Attacks are carefully organized and are preceded by propitiatory rites. First of all, scouts are sent to spy on the unsuspecting enemy, ascertain his battle potential, and decide on the best moment to strike, which is usually at dawn or sunset. The objective is the livestock enclosure: once the gates are opened, a select group gathers the animals together and runs off as quickly as possible, protected by a cordon of warriors whose job is to ward off any reaction on the part

of the victims. During their retreat, the booty is divided equally among the participants in the raid. Their arrival in the village is triumphal, celebrated with great festivities and cries of exultation on the part of the women. The Borana social system, the *gada*, attaches great importance to the figure of the warrior and military skill. The *gada* is based on stratification by generations: the passage from one level to another, which is sanctioned by special rites, occurs every eight years and entails occupying a precise role in the hierarchy. A child's entrance into the *gada* depends on the age class of his father, regardless of his date of birth. There are eleven levels in this social ladder and they mark a man's life from his infancy on. In keeping with custom, entrance into public life coincides with the granting of a name. Going up the social ladder means being recognized fit for caring for the livestock, then for using weapons, and later for marriage and the administration of justice. Circumcision takes place at the age of 48. The top level is that of the elder, whose authority is recognized by everyone. Those who reach this final stage of the *gada* are distinguished for their wisdom, seriousness and equanimity even in moments of great stress and crisis: they speak slowly in a low voice, using an initiatory language. As a power system the *gada* has lost part of its value but still has noteworthy symbolic weight and effectiveness. Thanks to the vigor of their traditions, the identity and unity of the Borana people have remained intact through the centuries.

ETHIOPIA 2003/04
"OMO VALLEY"

...THE ONLY ONES WHO HAND DOWN THE GLORIOUS TRADITIONS OF THEIR ANCESTORS:

THEY CALL THEMSELVES THE CHILDREN OF DAWN, THE FAVORITES OF WAQ, THE SUPREME GOD.

Borana women are considered among the most beautiful in all Ethiopia

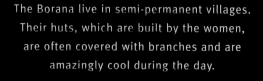

The Borana live in semi-permanent villages.
Their huts, which are built by the women,
are often covered with branches and are
amazingly cool during the day.

A shepherd rests with his grazing flock at the village entrance. At right is a gigantic termite hill, a typical sight in this region.

THE LAND OF HERDS
THE WATERWAY

322-323 The road to the 'Singing Wells'
is usually used to take the livestock to
pasture or to drink.

324-325 Traditionally women take care
of the dromedaries and are encharged of
transporting the water to the village.

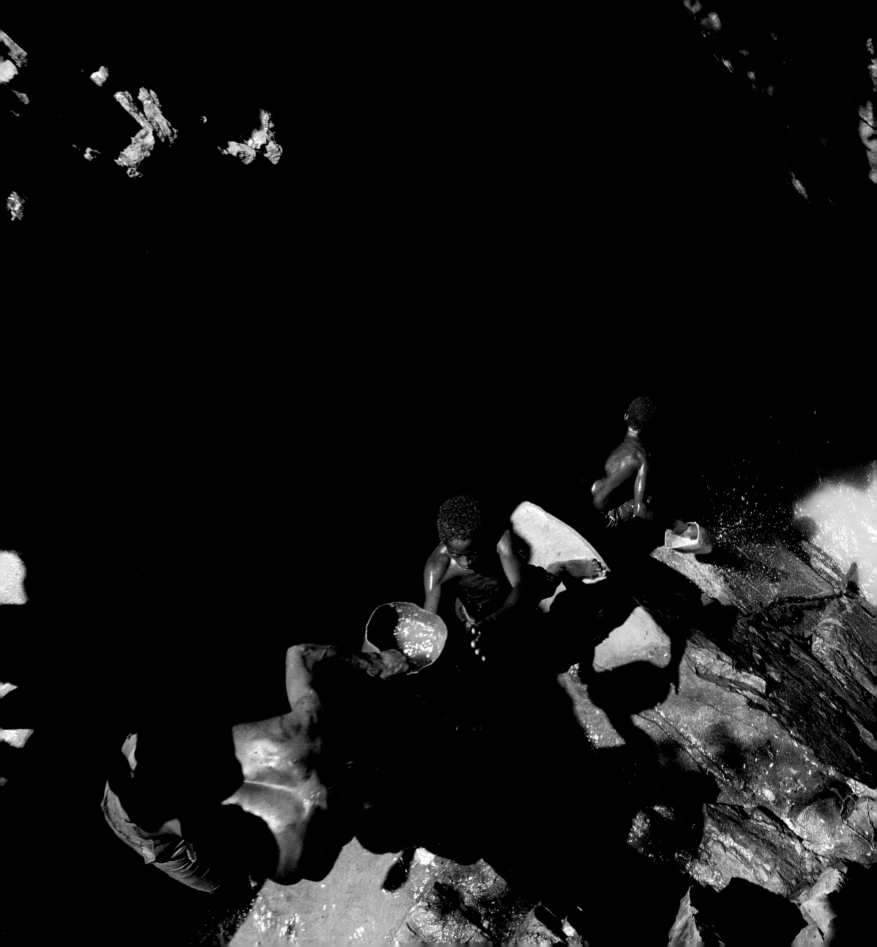

SINGING WELLS

IN THE DEPTHS OF THE EARTH

Inside the wells are the men
on natural platforms, passing
buckets filled with water.

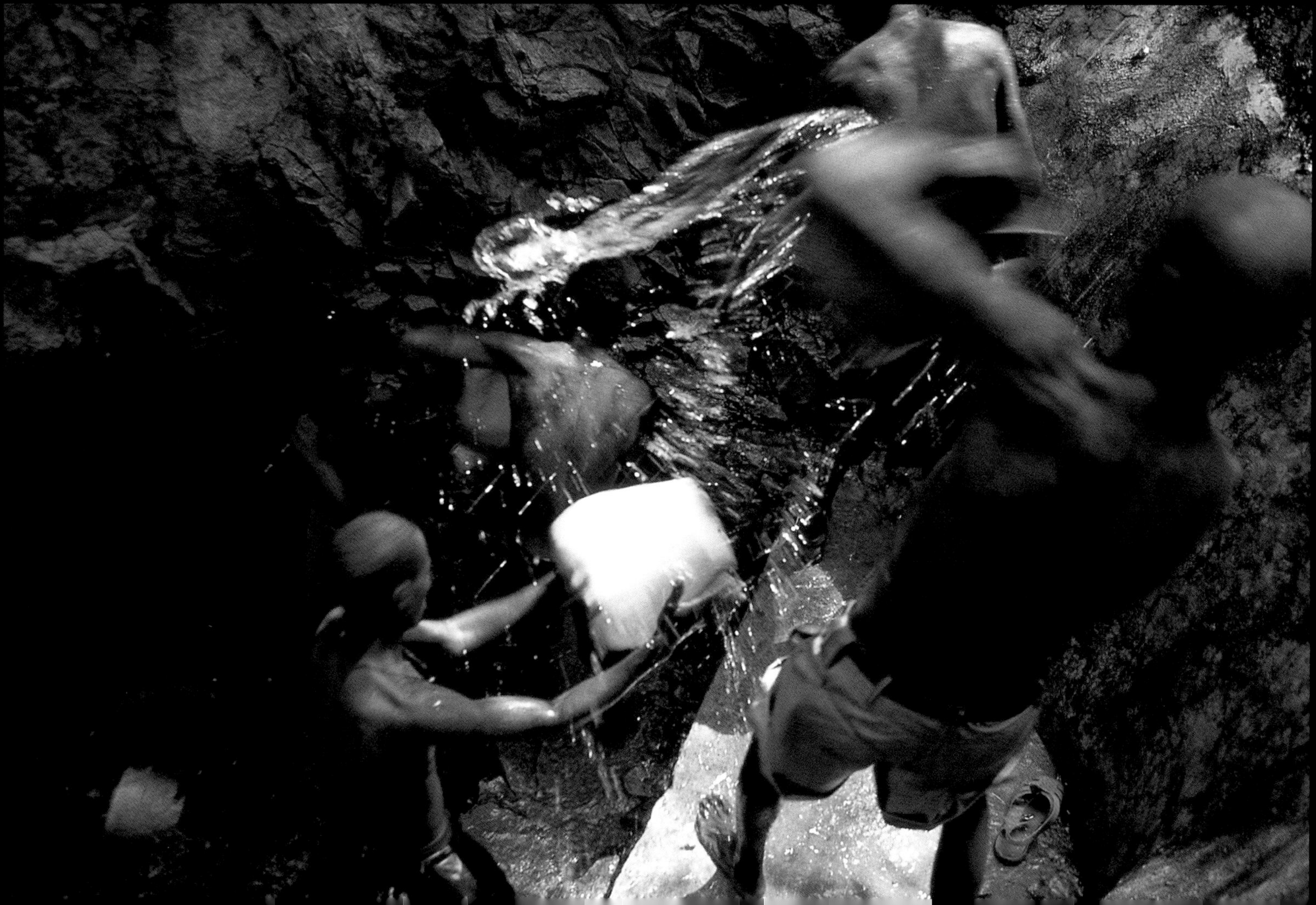

328 and 329 The men's work is accompanied by songs, which the Borana learn when they
are babies: this custom has given rise to the name 'Singing Wells' given to the site.

The work is hard and the men spend hours
in the freezing water of the spring.

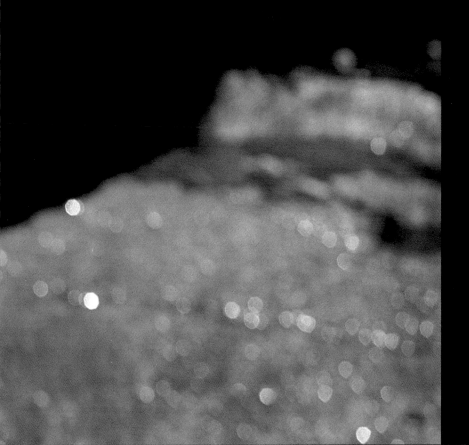

From a natural platform of the 'Singing Wells,' a young
man raises his head toward the light. The deepest
well known to date is about 130 feet deep.

EL SOD BORANA

LIFE IN THE VOLCANO

THE PAVED ROAD LEADS STRAIGHT TO MOYALE, THE LAST TOWN BEFORE THE KENYA BORDER. ONCE AT DUBLOCK, A TRACK 7.5 MILES (12 KM) LONG TAKES US DIRECTLY TO THE LARGEST SALT DEPOSIT IN ETHIOPIA, EL SOD.

The village of the Borana ethnic group lies right on the crest of a volcano that has been dormant for centuries, known as the House of Salt (Chew Bit): inside its crater a lake has formed that houses a veritable treasure for those who live in this area. Driven by curiosity, we decide to visit the lake.

Attracted by the din made by Paolo's arrival, a crowd of little boys surrounds our car to show us their humble wares, hoping that we'll buy something: small necklaces, aluminum objects, canes. Further along, two men seated under a straw-roof porch are chewing *chat*; every so often one of them stretches out his hand and offers a small branch to a goat grazing in front of them.

Seeing that we will purchase nothing, two of the boys offer to be our guides to the bottom of the crater. We begin to descend along a wide, dusty path. The lake, right below us, is so black that it looks like an enormous cup of coffee. After a few hairpin bends the walk becomes more difficult; stones have replaced the earth and the sound of the mules' hooves marks the rhythm of our march.

The large depression of the volcano is filled with green trees and shrubs that are proof of the abundant rainfall that characterizes this period of the year. The level of the lake is also higher; while many men extract salt here during the dry season, during this season only a few, the most expert, persevere in this work. The shores have white streaks, while thin reddish furrows mingle with the black color of the lake to create an almost lunar effect. At the bottom aof the crater some nude men seated next to the mules in a clearing are carefully covering part of their bodies with multicolored rags; in fact, the salt in the lake would be extremely painful on any exposed wounds or cuts. After rubbing balsam on their sores as protection, they dress them very carefully, one by one.

With only a few rags on them, their nude bodies on display without any sense of shame or embarrassment, the men go slowly toward the shore and go into the dark water with colored plastic containers in their hands: another workday has begun. Working in couples, they poke at the bottom with long poles to remove blocks of salt and then dive into the water to gather them. When they surface they are holding a black mass in their hands much like slime, which they place in floating tubs.

The sun is now high overhead and the morning passes by to the rhythm of the hustle and bustle of

A tired look, irritated eyes, and a face covered with white salt are the results of the fatiguing work at the El Sod volcano

these men, who take turns bringing the salt they have gathered to the shore to let it dry in the sun.

The silence of this huge open area is interrupted every once a while by short, precise orders from the older men, after which nothing more is heard.

I keep looking at a couple, father and son: up to their necks in the water, they dive down in turn and very slowly fill their tub with that miraculous catch. Swimming as best they can, they reach the shore and, barely keeping their balance, they dump the heavy load: a quick movement and they fling that shapeless mass onto the ground to dry. Those naked men in the water seem to have been generated by the volcano

and draw their lifeblood from its bowels.

The fatigue of the climb back up the slopes of the volcano with that suffocating heat clouds my vision, but in my mind I still have a clear image of the father and son with white spots on their skin, traces of salt that has dried in the sun.

When we are a few bends away from the top, a woman on the edge of the crater suddenly begins to shout toward the lake. Perhaps it is only a trivial message, but should those words ever be heard so far away, I would like to think that she is the wife and mother of those two sons of the Earth and is expressing all her love for them.

El Sod

The house of salt

336-337 Two men lead two salt-laden donkeys along the path. The El Sod crater is the largest salt deposit in Ethiopia.

338-339 The salt is piled up on the shore and left to dry: when dry, it is packed into canvas sacks.

Father and son scrape the black salt with long
sticks, then they bring it to the banks in large tubs.

VORACIOUS SALT

ENDURING SORES TO MAKE A LIVING

The constant contact with salt from El Sod causes ulcers and sores on the feet of these man that gather it

BORANA HANDS
RAG SALVES

The rags used to cover and soothe wounds
are the only remedy used against the salt's
caustic side-effects.

CROSSROAD OF PEOPLES

THE
GALEB

THE LAKE PEOPLE

THE GALEB

THE LAKE PEOPLE

T HE JOURNAL OF TELEKI'S EXPEDITION GIVES THE DHAASSANAC THE NAME THE RESHIAT. IN ETHIOPIA AND KENYA, THOSE WITH DARK SKIN ARE STILL FOR THE MOST PART KNOWN BY THE DEROGATORY NAME OF SHANGHILLA, OR NEGROES.

The term Galeb, which the Italians have transformed into the more familiar Gheleba, has the same meaning, while the Turkana call them Merille or Marille. The 19th-century explorers and the first ethnologists were at once the originators and victims of this confusion, and the difficulties in translation and pronunciation did the rest. The result is evident: there are at least 22 ethnonyms or names for ethnic groups, with their variations. To further complicate this situation is the fact that the Galeb are not a distinct ethnic group but rather an aggregate of populations with common values and traditions.

Each of the eight sections constituting the society, which is organized on a territorial basis, has different origins. The Ri'ele have Borana ancestry, the Randal are closely connected to the Rendille in northern Kenya, as are the Koro to the Masai, the Nartich to the Nyangatom, and so forth. The Inkabelo and Inkoria, who hail from lands that extend west of Lake Turkana, consider themselves "true Galeb," the primary stock around which the other groups gradually gathered. They are certainly the most numerous and occupy the best land. We don't know when this process of assimilation began, but von Honel and Teleki in the 19th century had already noted that the Galeb preferred foreigners as wives: the Samburu women were appreciated for their beauty and the children resulting from these mixed marriages were considered to be of noble lineage. The dissident factions of other tribes and exiles are still accepted and assimilated into the social system without too many problems. The above-mentioned pattern depends on one's residence and is not a hermetically sealed organism, whereas membership in a family clan is permanent and members are endowed with special ritual powers both in times of peace and war. Each clan has a specialization, which may range from prayer to more concrete duties such as protecting the herds while fording the river. The clans are also responsible for the preparation of the highly important ceremony of the *dimi*, a complex task that requires a lot of time and the combined efforts of different spiritual practitioners. The *dimi* sanctions the passage of girls into puberty: once circumcised, between the ages of eight to ten, the girls can become mothers and guarantee the continuity of the tribe. This event concerns only the first-born daughters,

Two women's curiosity is aroused by the arrival of foreigners.

who receive the solemn benediction of the elders, which ensures future fertility.

But the true protagonists of the festivities are the fathers, who on this occasion reach the top of the social ladder. From this moment on they no longer have to bother about contingent, ephemeral problems but concentrate on politics and administration. However, the rise to this position entails a heavy price to pay: each participant in the *dimi* has to sacrifice ten bulls and at least thirty goats and sheep. The animals are butchered and their meat distributed among the members of the clan. This is tantamount to eliminating in one stroke all one's assets, accumulated with hard work and sacrifices during the course of a lifetime. The ceremony, marked by banquets, dances and libations, may last up to six weeks. The men show off their best clothing, decorating their heads with ostrich feathers and hanging cheetah and monkey skins over their shoulders. A wooden shield and phallus-shaped cane round out their "outfit," which must not be much different from the one used many years earlier during the circumcision rite.

For the Galeb the male initiation rite takes place at a rather late age, around thirty, and has paradoxical features. In the passage from adolescence to adulthood the boy dresses up like a woman, totally imitating female behavior: he wears a skirt and female ornaments and plays with children in a loving manner. The people in the village treat him with great delicacy, satisfy his every whim and feed him specially prepared food, as is done with a young mother. For unknown reasons, the result of this kind of sweet and delicate upbringing will be a fierce warrior able to slit the throat of an enemy with the cold indifference of a professional killer. The Galeb are the scourge of the neighboring populations. They have an abundance of weapons and know how to use them. Their custom of castrating their enemies adds a sinister tone to their exploits in thievery. They make cyclical rustling raids against the Nyangatom, Hamer, Gabbra, Rendille, Turkana and whoever else has livestock for the taking.

Their territory extends to the north and east of Lake Turkana, on either bank of the Omo River. There are about 32,000 Galeb in Ethiopia, and the groups that live in Kenya number a few thousand. This region is basically arid and beaten by strong winds, and the average temperature is about 40 °C. Rainfall is scarce and erratic, often preceded by nerve-wracking dust storms that blanket the horizon for days and days. The relative prosperity of the Galeb in this harsh and cruel environment stems from the existence of permanent sources of water that are of easy access. Thanks to this abundance of water, agriculture is a profitable enterprise: sorghum, corn and beans are grown in the fertile alluvial land next to the river, which is subject to regular seasonal flooding. The level of the Omo's waters does not depend on local meteorological conditions but rather on the rains that fall in the highlands hundreds of miles away, so that even when there is long-term drought locally, a good harvest is almost always guaranteed.

The right to exploit the land is established by means of flexible rules: in critical periods the earth is used for grazing, while at other times it is plowed and sown, on a rotating basis. This system ensures the survival of at least some of the livestock while also retaining at least

The harshness of the land is reflected in the hollow cheeks and bony features of this man.

some of the agricultural products. In any case, the public good has priority over private property. Farmers out of necessity, the Galeb basically consider themselves a pastoralist population. Typical features of pastoral societies are the values that guide their behavior, the rites, the organization into age classes, and the high respect paid to their herds. Meat is rarely a part of their diet because killing an animal is tantamount to squandering one's riches. Like many other ethnic groups in southern Ethiopia, they bleed their cows; the blood, mixed with milk, is considered a tid-

bit and is used as an "instant" energizer. Although fishing is systematically practiced, it is considered a base occupation. Equally unworthy for men are manual labor and commerce (which in any case is limited to very few articles such as tobacco, tea, sugar and other luxury items). Isolated as they are from the outside world, in the middle of one of the most inaccessible and turbulent areas in Africa, the Galeb continue to live in keeping with their traditions. Nothing in modern civilization seems to interest them except automatic firearms.

ETHIOPIA 2003/04
"OMO VALLEY"

...THE MAN WHO TOOK US ACROSS THE RIVER IN HIS BOAT IS NOTHING MORE OR LESS THAN AN AFRICAN CHARON WHO HAS FERRIED US TO DANTE'S INFERNO...

Like many other tribes in the Omo Valley, the Galeb decorate their bodies with iron earrings and bracelets and glass bead necklaces

GALEB

TRAVEL NOTES

T HE TWO BANKS OF THE RIVER ARE SEPARATED BY CENTURIES. AT LEAST THIS IS THE IMPRESSION ONE HAS. ACTUALLY, BETWEEN RATE AND THE GALEB VILLAGE OF OMORATE THERE IS ONLY THE OMO, NOT MORE THAN 165 FEET (50 M) OF RIVERBED. BUT THE DISTANCE IS IMMENSE.

After leaving the car at Rate, we go down the slope to the bank, where a kind of boat is waiting to take us across the Omo. The landscape is harmonious. The green of the trees is bright and the vegetation luxuriant. The brown of the embankment contrasts with the river, which at this point seems to be blue. The animals go there to drink and the women, after washing their clothes, go back up the bank, walking erectly with huge baskets on their heads. The oars of the few solitary wooden pirogues produce reflections on the water. Everything contributes to creating a sensation of quiet and sweetness that unfortunately soon comes to an end. When we arrive at the other side and give instructions to the boatman, we ascend, and a little more than 100 yards or so from the shore, catch sight of the village. Three or four persons come toward us and we immediately realize that they are different from the men in any other tribe: they are terribly emaciated, use canes to walk with, and have a sad look that may be desperate or even blank. All around there is only dust,

torrid heat and barrenness. Not even one tree to provide a bit of shade and a place to rest, not one enclosure or one animal. There is nothing in this place.

We arrive in the middle of the village: even the children, who are usually so lively and enterprising, merely watch us in amazement, move around and talk very little, and hardly ever smile. Among the huts are two elderly women with strange headdresses and extremely long canes; they talk in a very low voice and walk slowly and aimlessly. Two men are absorbed in cleaning and sharpening knives and arrowheads: primitive weapons. Unlike the rest of Ethiopia, here there are no Kalashnikovs. Another man, who may be the village chief, has a whip in his hand and chases the children, who now move in front of my lens. While I am taking pictures of them, a large scorpion climbs up my camera's videotape magazine. Perhaps it's the effect of the scorching heat, but the people I see before me begin to look like souls wandering in a circle of Hell, damned without any hope of salvation. Only a few yards away there is water, the river, shade, a world in movement. Yet it seems that the Galeb are chained to their desert of dust, as if an invisible, impassable borderline blocked their way.

Unexpectedly and suddenly our journey undergoes a transformation. The man who took us across the river in his boat is nothing more or less than an

355 Unlike the other Omo Valley populations, the Galeb use only spears and arrows as weapons.

356-357 The children at Rate spend the afternoon playing in the shade to gain shelter from the scorching sun

African Charon who has ferried us to Dante's Inferno, while our guide Zinabu, knowledge-able about the places and customs, is our trustworthy Virgil who accompanies us and provides us with all the answers we need. Then a breath of air, a sudden breeze carries away the sensation of being in a place far from the real world, and things and persons again take on their materiality. Working in this place means experiencing all its desola-tion, so much so that when it's unbearably hot you actually believe you are in the bor-derland of humanity.

We stay at the village more than four hours, then go back down to the river. While we are leaving, accompanied by our Charon, I'm surprised by the feeling of relief at think-ing about civilization – which consists of a bar and a jeep – that awaits us on the other side of the river.

This is the hottest hour of the day.
At Rate the children and animals find shade
in the village huts made of hides and bark.

360-361 The chief of the village of Rate giving his fellow villagers instructions concerning the day's chores.

361 With their spears and jars, two women cross through the village on their way to the river to draw water.

The rhythm of the life of the Galeb is typical of a pastoral society.

From 364 to 367 Despite the fact that they have grown up in a rather poor environment, the Galeb girls pay special attention to their appearance and adorn themselves with many strings of colored glass beads and metal bracelets.

THE MYSTERIOUS RESIDENTS OF THE MAGO RIVER

THE
KARO

FRESCOES
ON THE SKIN

[PAOLO NOVARESIO]

THE KARO

FRESCOES ON THE SKIN

T HE KARO (ALSO CALLED KERE, CHERRE AND KERRE) LIVE IN THE LOWER OMO RIVER REGION, SOUTH OF CONFLUENCE WITH THE MAGO RIVER.

This ethnic group is small, numbering a few hundred persons scattered in a handful of villages that are connected by mule tracks that are hard to negotiate even with four-wheel drive. Duss, a half-day's journey from the Mago National Park, is the oldest and most important Karo settlement.

Little is known about this population. Ethnologists have never studied Karo society in depth and what has been written about them is based on sketchy, almost always second-hand information. Even the last census taken by the Ethiopian government in 1994, which adopted rigorous methods and was quite meticulous, totally ignored the Karo, assimilating them with the Hamer. The former have a close relationship of clientage with their more powerful neighbors that has been codified by age-old tradition. The Karo language belongs to the Omotic group and 80% of it is similar to that of the Hamer; but many Karo also speak Nyangatom. The Karo also have a series of customs, rituals and religious beliefs, as well as the economic system, in common with the Hamar. Even the clothing and symbolic meaning of scarification coincide to an amazing degree, thus

suggesting a common historic and cultural background. A mysterious relationship links the Karo to the Mogudji and Kwegu, two small ethnic groups that live in the Mago River Valley; indeed, the Kwegu and Karo often life side by side in the same village and intertribal marriages are frequent.

Nonetheless, the Karo, despite the obvious relations with the neighboring peoples, claim an original identity for themselves. This desire for differentiation is expressly mostly in how they paint their bodies, which becomes a true art form. In Africa and elsewhere painting one's face and other parts of the body with mineral or plant pigments is common practice and meets spiritual, social or purely aesthetic needs. The different use of patterns and colors transmits a system of symbolic messages, indicating the individual's position in the group, access to rites of passage from one age class to another, or the killing of an enemy in battle. By the same token, body painting highlights the beauty of the individual's features and the harmony of the physique, communicating the joy of living, strength and health.

Together with ocher, yellow and lime, the Karo make frequent use of black, which is got from charcoal or from ferrous stones that are pulverized and diluted with water. All these substances are readily available in the region. The decoration, effected

A group of women standing on the promontory that overlooks the bend in the Omo River close to their village.

with scraped and smoothed sticks and other occasional tools, is extremely accurate and takes several hours to finish, especially when dances and important ceremonies are concerned. Geometric motifs are flanked by signs representing birds' plumage, in particular that of wild guinea fowl. Then the entire body, from head to toe, is covered with white dots, making a startling visual impact. Straight lines, zigzags, small circles, stars, handprints – the fantasy of the Karo is boundless and often the men prove to be more enterprising in this than the women. A white ostrich feather, the symbol of purity and courage, is placed on the colored clay that covers the nape of warriors' necks. Glass beads, once imported from Europe by Arab traders and used for bartering, are very much appreciated: they are threaded and make for elaborate necklaces that go with the others made of seeds of the *ensete* (a relative of the banana) and other plants. Equally popular are cowries, tiny shells from the Indian Ocean whose shape inevitably reminds the viewer of the vagina. There are also many lip ornaments made of thin metal rods of different length: even a common nail set into the lower lip may have a function.

Physical beauty is extremely important among the Karo: neglecting to care for personal appearance, especially when young, is inconceivable and results in tacit exclusion from social life. To be is to appear, and during the festivities held after harvest or on occasion of weddings, ostentation of elegance is a must, a necessity, if a man wants to find a wife.

The Karo grow sorghum but integrate their agricultural activities with fishing and sheep and goat breeding. Over a century ago, the American explorer Donaldson Smith was struck by their dignity and self-esteem and by the abundance of food in the region. He could not help noticing that the Karo did not like intruders in their land and were feared by their neighbors for their military prowess. However, in peacetime they led a quiet life; the daily tasks, carried out in morning to avoid the torrid heat, left plenty of time for idleness, conversing and social activities.

For several decades the situation has been drastically changed. The massive use of firearms in the lower Omo region has greatly altered the rules of the game, so to speak, creating a state of permanent tension. Not only do the Karo run the risk of being physically overpowered by their more numerous and better armed neighbors, but their very lifestyle is jeopardized. The territorial borders established by custom are becoming more and more unstable under the pressure brought to bear by other more vigorous tribes in desperate search of new grazing land. Tourism, a new phenomenon in southern Ethiopia, has worsened this state of affairs, creating serious cultural traumas: the Karo now dance and allow themselves to be photographed for money, selling their very identity for a few dollars. Impoverished and weakened, brutally torn from the isolation that had protected them for centuries, they now risk cultural extinction. And yet, as if indifferent to their destiny, they stubbornly maintain their ancestral customs. Colorfully dressed, they smile at their uncertain future.

...belt of bullets and elaborate body painting, the Karo are masters in the art of decking themselves out.

…A WHITE OSTRICH FEATHER, THE SYMBOL OF PURITY AND COURAGE, IS PLACED ON THE COLORED CLAY THAT COVERS THE NAPE OF WARRIORS' NECKS.

Glass beads and nails: the beauty of the Karo women also consists of color and pain.

[GIANNI GIANSANTI]

THE BLACK MADONNA

ZERI'S GLANCE

THE JEEP MOVES LABORIOUSLY ON THE TRACK BARELY MARKED BY TWO LONG PARALLEL SPACES IN THE TALL VEGETATION. I move to the roof of the Toyota, seated on a tire between two cans of gasoline, in an attempt to indicate the exact direction of this indistinct passage, using the umbrella acacias scattered throughout this stretch of savanna as markers. Our car creates a large opening in the grass, which then rises up again in elegant waves after we have passed through, leaving its unique scent in the air. Labouk, Duss and Korcho are the only Karo villages in this territory that skirts the Omo River: 450 or perhaps 500 inhabitants including the men, women and children – no one knows the exact number. When the last members have disappeared there will remain no trace of the Karo ethnic group, one of the most fascinating in the entire valley.

At Labouk, the first village you come to when arriving from Mago National Park, some natives come to meet us, greeting us by raising one arm while firmly grasping their Kalashikovs with the other. After the customary introductions, we discuss with the village chief the possibility of staying overnight, setting up our tents among their huts. However, our guide Zinabu does not agree, and since he is the only one able to converse with the Karo, he persuades them to take us on a reconnaissance along the river bank. The place is too wild for a camp and I cannot even imagine the confusion and movement that prevail when night falls. And then, the river is so close by and is full of crocodiles. So I suggest, or rather almost insist, that we go back to the village and make an agreement with the Karo, so that I can photograph everything that occurs there. Zinabu and Anaylem look at me with a withering glance, insisting that we cannot sleep in the village; but thanks to Paolo's mediation, we obtain permission to stay all the same.

A few faint smiles, some dirty looks and a hyena in the guise of a woman are our company that sunny afternoon, which is hot and teeming with insects. In fact, there are so many that we eat a frugal meal more quickly than usual in order to return hastily to the shelter of our tents. Three Karo warriors armed with rifles lie on humble straw pallets on the ground, where they will guard the camp in the firelight.

378-379 Zeri is staring into the distance: she gave birth only a few hours ago.

Upon awakening, I open our tent and the dawn appears with the sky covered with leaden clouds through which I catch a glimpse of the first rays of sunlight. I leave my world to enter theirs, while one of the guards nods in greeting and watches me as I walk away. I begin a rapid tour of the village, which is still wrapped in sleep, and take the first photos of an old woman, who seems to be the village chief's wife, while she loads two empty gasoline cans on her curved back and heads toward the river to get some water. I go back to the tents where, in the meantime, Zinabu and Anaylem have awakened. I ask them if everything is all right. "Yes, Gianni, everything is OK!" They seem to be sincere, and in any case are more relaxed: at breakfast I finally see Anaylem smile. The worst is over with, part of the past.

Unlike other ethnic groups such as the Surma or Mursi, who live in the forest, the Karo live by the river, which is the reason why I decided to photograph them while they navigate down the Omo in their tree-trunk pirogues. Standing upright, so elegant in their multicolored livery freely drawn on the their bodies, with the aid of long poles they move upstream in the muddy river water, passing by large sorghum fields. It is late morning when we take our

leave of the tribal chief and his warriors, thanking them for their hospitality. Even the woman-hyena, who lambasted me with swear words every time I pointed the lens of my camera at her, seems more mild, or at least less wild.

All of sudden, on our way back along the track, among the dry bushes of a field there appears the figure of a woman wrapped in a cloth that in turn swathes a newborn child. She has a stare that fades away into the horizon. I move around her, take pictures of her, and smile at her. She seems imperturbable. Between her arms I catch a glimpse of a baby's tiny head, with wet hair, against her mother's breast. "Her name is Zeri and she has just given birth," Zinabu whispers in my ear in order not to disturb the woman. Very slowly I take a couple of steps backward. I look at her while moving away, and one thought troubles me: I'm afraid I may have disturbed her with my presence and with the metallic sound of my camera.

For days the vision of that black Madonna, as statuesque as a Pietà with Mary holding the crucified Christ, will remain vivid in my mind as living proof of the suffering that prevails in these areas, and in Africa.

KORCHO
ON THE BEND OF THE OMO RIVER

380 In the Karo territory the Omo River is indeed a grandiose spectacle.

381 This aerial view of Korcho, which has barely one hundred inhabitants, shows how small the village is.

382-383 In order to protect his cattle from rustlers, a cowherd keeps watch from a rise.

384-385 Some boys reconnoitering the river in dugouts.

THE CEREMONY OF COLLECTION

SORGHUM, THE KAROS' FOOD

386-387 Sorghum, which is grown in fields
not far from the village, is a staple of the
Karo diet.

388-389 The men use large machetes to cut
the cane, which has a very pleasant sweet
taste.

390 and 391 The women participate in the harvest of the sorghum up to the threshing.

392-393 This man's tired face is framed by a landscape consisting of grass yellowed by the sun and huts with conical roofs.

394 The young women are usually entrusted with caring for the elderly members of their group.

395 As throughout the whole Omo Valley, even among the Karo women have very heavy chores.

396-397 Kalashnikovs, one of which is seen here hanging from the hut like a common household
object, are also part and parcel of the Karo lifestyle.

398 Knotted hair comprises the typical hairdo of Karo women.

399 With a dour expression, this man shows the scarification on his chest

400-401 The torrid midday heat forces the families to take long, refreshing rests in their huts.

The women prepare lunch—a freshly
slaughtered kid goat.

These young males paint their
bodies with patterns that are
often nothing more or less
than their handprints.

Kalashnikovs, shoulder belts and colored fabrics are the usual 'outfit' of Karo men.

...STRAIGHT LINES, ZIGZAGS, SMALL CIRCLES, STARS, HANDPRINTS–THE FANTASY OF THE KARO IS BOUNDLESS AND OFTEN THE MEN PROVE TO BE MORE ENTERPRISING IN THIS THAN THE WOMEN.

The elaborate grooming of the Karo, often consisting of body painting, requires much care and attention.

The Karo
Timeless warriors

410-411 The Karo obtain the colors needed
for their body painting by mixing plant
pigments and clay.

412-413 The men gather together their hair
in special hairdos set with clay: while
waiting for it to dry, they sleep on their
borkota, which are special wooden
headrests.

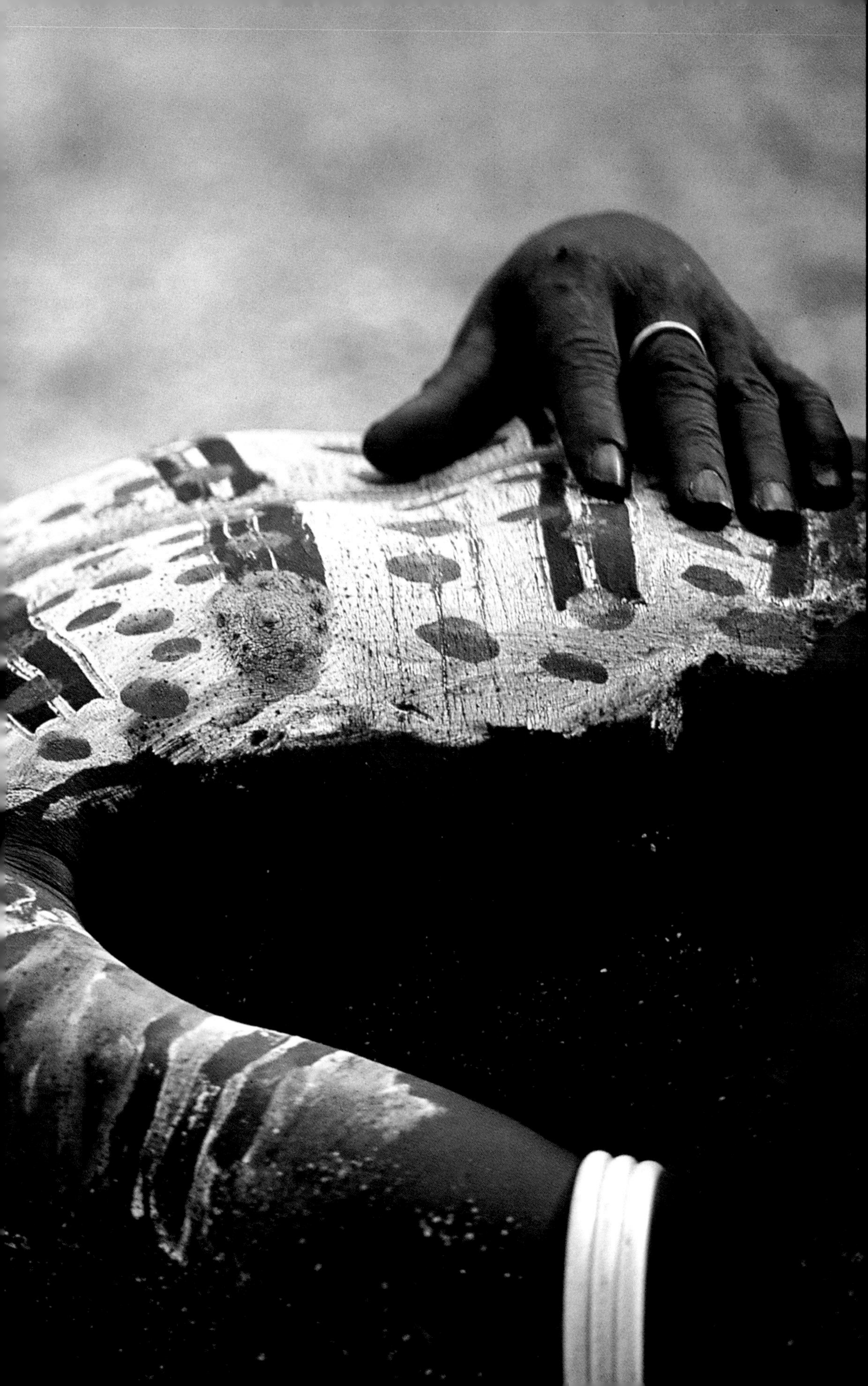

THE PEOPLES OF THE PLANES

THE HAMER

PRIDE AND BEAUTY

THE HAMER

PRIDE AND BEAUTY

Beyond the Woito River Valley the landscape suddenly changes: the last declivities of the highlands disappear, as if swallowed up by the boundless plains that extend as far as the eye can see toward the Kenya border.

The hills and cultivated fields of the Land of Konso give way to savannas and scrub; only a few isolated rises break the monotony of the horizon. The huts of the Hamer are the only sign of civilization in this wild setting. The arrangement of the villages, which seem to be scattered helter-skelter in the prairie, is actually in keeping with a well detailed mental map that takes account the needs of a mixed economy based on livestock and agriculture. The crops are usually planted near wells, and at the same time the pastures must not be too far away from the villages. The Hamer settled in their present territory fairly recently. Their history and mythology speak of a glorious past when their original ancestors decided to live on the tops of mountains. And their oral tradition tells us that they were the first to use fire and originate the Hamer lineage: light emanated from the flames as tall as a star in the dark sky and attracted people from everywhere, including the Konso, Ari, Tsamai, Karo, Male and Bume peoples. They all swore to be obedient and respectful and thus became

Hamer. To this day the Hamer regard fire as a regenerating force, the symbol of the beginning of everything. When someone dies the brazier is put out and its rekindling is accompanied by elaborate benedictions. After the harvest the stubbles are burned so that their ashes can give new strength to the Earth. And the word "inflamed" is used to describe a person gifted with energy and creativity.

Indeed, this legend has a basis of truth: the Hamer are the result of the mixture of different groups who immigrated from neighboring tribes that centuries ago took refuge on the rises northwest of Lake Turkana. The American Donaldson Smith, who visited the area in 1895, met them not far from the shores of Lake Stefanie. A squad of warriors tried to rob him but their attack was easily thwarted. At that time firearms had not yet made their appearance in southern Ethiopia but the region was in turmoil because of large-scale tribal conflict. A long time before European explorers arrived in the zone the Hamer had checked the advance of the Borana at the Woito River; after bitter fighting they gained victory thanks to magic, as they flung swarms of furious bees on the terrorized invaders. After the Borana there came masses of Samburu and then the Turkana, who retreated in haste, leaving death and devastation in their wake. But the real trouble was yet to come.

417 The village of Dambaite lies in the heart of a verdant valley.

420-421 The elderly Haylo holds the spear he inherited from his brother Beldembe, who in turn received it as a gift from the Bume.

422-423 Sopy takes a peek at the coffee ritual taking place in the hut.

The division of Africa among the colonial powers had begun and the Ethiopian Empire was involved against its will. At the end of 1900, in order to check British expansionism, Emperor Menelik II sent his troops to conquer the borderland with Kenya. His large and well-armed army quickly defeated the Hamer, who were armed only with spears. Many of them were killed or taken into slavery, others fled into the scrubland to lead a life of vagabondage. After their conquest, the Ethiopians armed the tribes of the south, encouraging them to make raids into northern Kenya. Italian colonization did not change this state of affairs. Hamer society maintained its integrity but was clearly upset by this whirl of events: pillage, once simple a means of accumulating riches, became the symbol of tribal honor and prestige. Parallel to this, the traditional structures were weakened. The semi-nomadic life in the arid lowlands increased the people's intolerance of every form of authority. Personal choices replaced those made for the commonweal. The character of the present-day Hamer reflects this vision of the world. The power of the chiefs and prominent persons is essentially ritual: their acts, like those of all religious and civic functionaries, are constantly checked and controlled by the *donza*, or married men. It is these latter more than anyone else who have the capacity to evoke the *barjo*, that is, the fortune and well-being innate in every human being, in nature, in places and even in inanimate objects. The

barjo may be interpreted as a kind of fundamental principle, the primal condition of the existence and harmony of the universe. Without *barjo* the sorghum would not grow, the rain would cease to fall and the universe itself, the Sun, the sky and the stars, would precipitate into chaos.

Man can consciously activate this invisible agent, awakening its power through songs and invocations, which duly precede the beginning of all meetings. The *barjo* increases with age, thus providing the elderly with a bland system of control over the youth and women in a society that is fundamentally anarchic and lacking in rigid moral constrictions. In fact, the words "sin," "shame," "honor" and "duty," as well as the concepts of absolute Good and Evil, simply do not exist in the Hamer vocabulary. Superstition, on the other hand, is quite widespread, hence the overwhelming presence of soothsayers, who are consulted in cases of serious illness or when a person suspects he/she is the victim of the evil eye. The most common illnesses are generally cured with the aid of herbs, roots and natural substances, which are either swallowed or rubbed on the aching part of the body. Failure on the part of traditional medicine is a sign of malediction, and other methods then have to be tried. The guilty party may be a relative or foreigner but may also be the spirit of a dead person unsatisfied with how he/she has been treated. In this case, in order to appease the spirit's anger an animal must be sacriticed: if the offering is sufficient the ghost will leave the village for ever and return to live in peace in its own world, beyond the Great Waters. However, the soothsayers may also use their influence for evil purposes, for example by urging the men to wage war, which is considered a form of madness. In this case it is up to the elders to limit their influence.

Lacking a stable center of gravity, as it were, the Hamer social system would seem to risk disintegration. But there is a series of mechanisms that guarantee this will not happen: for instance, the obligation to help relatives and those in difficulty, especially during drought or famine, is a strongly felt sentiment. The benefactor acquires fame and respect in the tribe and his virtues are publicly celebrated after his death. Furthermore, a loan, usually consisting of animals, is an investment of capital. The animals reproduce and a cow one has loaned may return to the owner with its accrued "interest." The fragmentation of assets has other advantages: it conceals a man's true wealth (which is ill-considered if put on display), reduces the risk of losing everything in one fell swoop (because of robbery, raids, epidemics) and, at least on a formal level, it makes the society more egalitarian and cohesive. The Hamer breed goats most of all, for unlike a herd of cattle or camels, these animals do not require collective management, which among the pastoralist populations is usually based on age groups. It is much more important to be mobile and

make quick decisions, gifts that are more suitable to a small independent group rather than a large and articulated organization. Cows are esteemed more for their intrinsic and ritual value than for their products. Like the neighboring Karo, Banna and Bashada, the young Hamer must go through the "Bull's Leap" initiation ceremony in order become full-fledged adults. This event is the occasion to make a show of one's beauty and elegance. The women's clothing is spectacular: metal collars, colored glass beads and bandoliers made of shells adorn the girls' bodies. They spread and mix ocher and animal fat on their hair in order make balls and plaits. An aluminum visor called a *kallé* juts out over the forehead and rows of bracelets underscore the rotundity of the girls' arms. Only married women can wear a *bignere* – a heavy iron band with a showy phallic protuberance – around their necks. The men show off their complex hairdos with ostrich feathers, while the inseparable wooden headrest is used to sit on as well as to protect the hairdo while they sleep. The aesthetic exuberance of the Hamer is expressed in their dances and festivities, which often brighten their daily life. The sound of the flute and lyre accompany the songs that narrate heroic exploits and wars, bless the fields, animals and nature, call for rain, and ward off misfortune. In these litanies the words are repeated, gathering strength and solidity: it is the human voice that creates the world anew every day.

[GIANNI GIANSANTI]

BARGHY

THE FACE OF CHANGING AFRICA

WHEN I RETURNED FROM MY FIRST TRIP TO ETHIOPIA, A FRIEND ASKED ME WHY I HAD GONE TO THAT PART OF AFRICA AND I TOLD HIM ABOUT BARGHY, WHO I THOUGHT WAS THE BEST EXAMPLE THAT COULD EXPLAIN THE MEANING OF MY PROJECT.

Barghy is a young Hamer. I met her for the first time at Hassafu's bar in Turmi, a sort of unexpected oasis for the few passing tourists. We had just finished the usual 6-7 hours of African track, with the usual holes and intolerable heat. She was with a group of children who upon our arrival immediately ran to us with the eternal refrain: "*Bir, bir,* hallo, *frenji,* hallo, photo...."

Barghy remained immobile, seated on a faded light blue bench under the straw kiosk, staring at us with a mixture of curiosity and surprise, her crossed hands on her dangling legs and red braids flowing down from her head. Immobile. In the midst of all the excitement and loud cries of the children who were having such fun, who were blocking my way, calling to me and asking me for money and gifts, I noticed only her unusual behavior, not participating in the merrymaking, not asking or calling or shouting.

The children did somersaults to attract my attention; Barghy remained still. The children waged mock battles, ran up and down the dusty street; Barghy remained still. With one hand the children lifted their torn T-shirts to show me the non-existent muscles of their chests, and with the other hand tried to pull up their oversize, buttonless trousers that slipped down with every step they took. Barghy settled gracefully on the bench, one hand on her goatskin dress decorated with pearls, the other holding up her chin. At a certain point her wide-open eyes flashed with a smile that gradually spread all over her face, revealing her shiny white teeth, her face bathed in the only ray of light filtering from the straw roof. Click.

This is what I came here for.

I understood this at that very moment. Naturally, I knew I was traveling in search of something, but I wasn't exactly sure what it was. And even if I knew, I wasn't sure I would find it. Barghy, with that gesture of hers, with her goatskin dress, her immobility in the midst of moving persons and things, had explained this to me without uttering a word. Better yet, Barghy had shown me what I had to do: crystallize in a fraction of a second the events that have been repeated since time immemorial in this part of the world.

Barghy, the Hamer who spent her afternoons at the bar with her friends from Turmi. Barghy with the goatskin dress who went to school with children who wore T-shirts with the Italian football player Totti's number and name on it. Two different

Barghy, a splendid Hamer girl, is the symbol of the times that have changed even in Africa.

ways of living with and confronting passing time: some try to keep up with it, others keep their distance from it. Click. When I saw Barghy again a couple of months later, I didn't recognize her. She was again at the bar in company with the uncontrollable children with their torn T-shirts. I knew I would find her here, yet I didn't recognize her. Not even when she approached me and said in a thin voice: "Ciao, Djiani."

Her head was clean-shaven and she too was wearing a pair of shorts and a man's cotton T-shirt that was too big for her and torn.

"Oh, ciao, Barghy. Nagaya". That's all I managed to say to her. "Oh, ciao, Barghy. Nagaya."

What I didn't manage to say to her was: "What have you done, Barghy? What's happened to you? Where are your Hamer braids, your Hamer necklaces and your Hamer goatskin dress? If it is true that clothing is the key to understanding your tradition, the element that distinguishes one tribe from another, tell me why you have decided not to be a Hamer any longer? What will you get by wearing a T-shirt and a pair of shorts? Is this a way to pursue and recover time? It is a way of regaining what you have lost?"

I think again about what vanished, lost gestures mean to me. I think about the aesthetic value and emotional meaning we give to everything that has passed and will never again return. I think of the comparison we usually make between what was and is no longer, and what will be....

Barghy has changed and will never again be like her former self....

I realize that I would like everything to stay exactly as it is in this part of Africa. I would like to hear that in this corner of the world speed, technology and progress are simply not envisaged. Here, where the only possibility of finding a cell phone is to see pieces of one attached to someone's neck as pendants; here, where precooked food packets become purses to carry on one's shoulder. I think that my photographs may satisfy a curiosity and desire that we all share: investigate the living past with the eyes of the present. That's it: perhaps we see ourselves in these people as we were thousands of years ago.

I don't know if Barghy made the right decision. I know that Barghy is a lovely Hamer girl who has decided to see what our world, so different from hers, is like. Some people tell me that it is better to continue to be a Hamer in Omo River Valley than a beggar in Adis Abeba. Others think that everyone should have the opportunity to change and "improve," and that stopping Barghy from doing so would be selfish on our part. Yet others think that if we didn't come here and show these people our jeeps, cameras and mobile phones, Barghy and her friends would not crave for them and everything would be infinitely better....

I've been told that in a short time they will build a paved road that goes as far as Turmi. This means more tourists, more money. Time will begin to fly and, skipping over all the transition stages, will leave behind it 2,000 years of immobile history. The Vanished Time of a Vanishing Africa.

Barghy: now grown up, she has become 'Westernized' in her clothes and hairdo.

428-429 Barghy: the innocence and beauty of a young Hamer girl.

er villages are extensive, since every family has a hut as well as an enclosure for the livestock

432-433 This woman with a
goatskin dress decorated with
shells is doing maintenance
work on her hut.

434-435 A girl from Arna is
about to milk a goat.

VENUS WITH A GUN

THE VIOLENT SIDE OF THE HAMER

This statuesque woman, who has braids and
decorative shells, is shouldering her rifle with
incredible self-assurance.

438-439 A woman from
Delaban tries to cool herself
in the water in this sort of
amphora.

440-441 Portrait of a family
in their home: the father,
mother, two children and the
few indispensable
household furnishings.

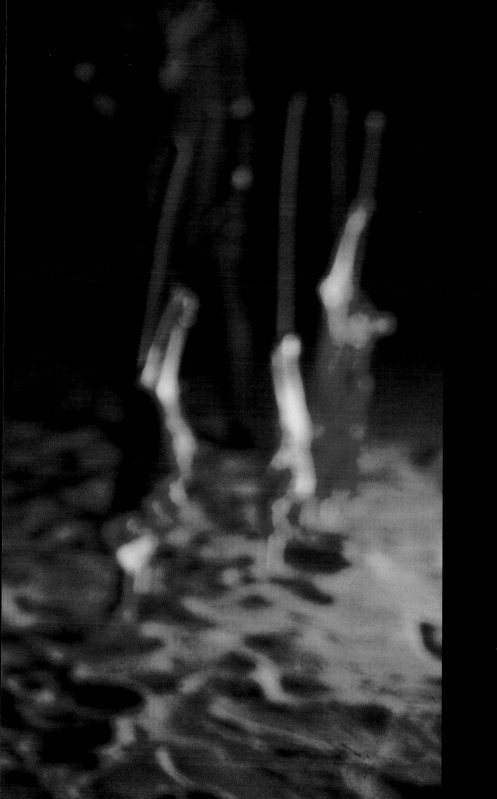

Late in the evening, illumin
some villagers get togethe
goat, one of the staples of

...THE HAIR IS GREASED WITH OCHER COLORING AND ANIMAL FAT THAT ARE MOLDED INTO BRAIDS AND LITTLE BALLS.

445 and 446-447 The combination of the elaborate braided hairdo, metal chokers, colored glass beads and shell shoulder belts make Hamer women particularly fascinating

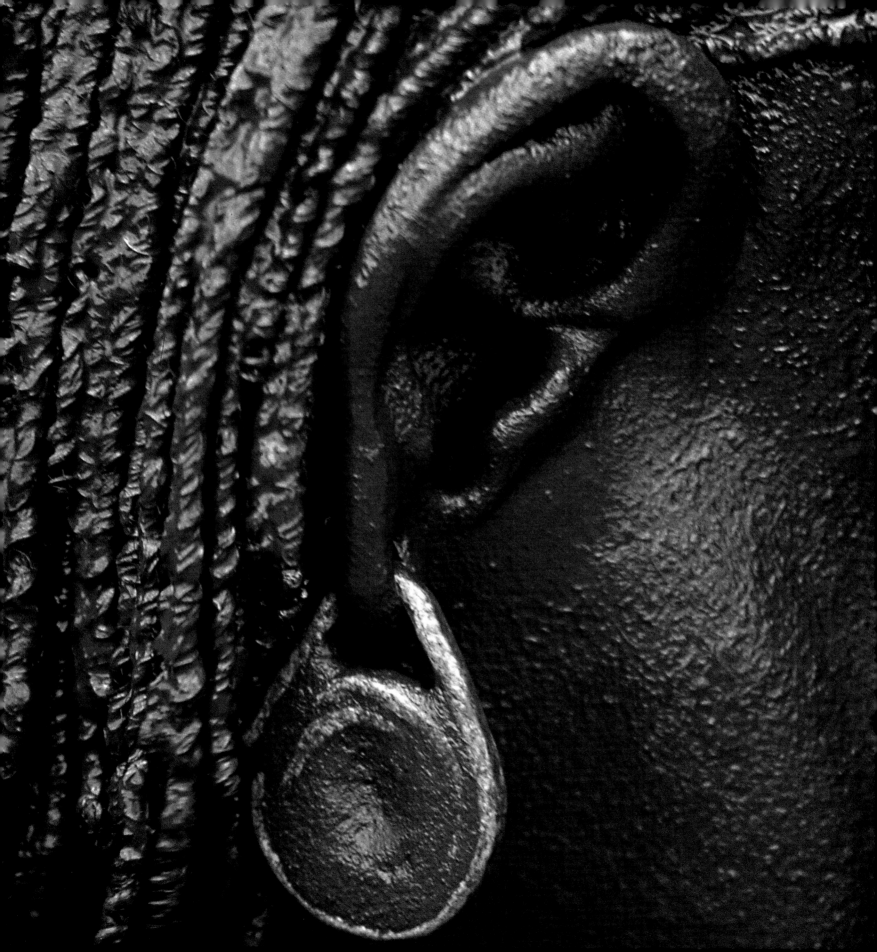

This young woman's glance expresses all the pride and curiosity of her Hamer sisters.

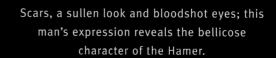

Scars, a sullen look and bloodshot eyes; this
man's expression reveals the bellicose
character of the Hamer.

The sun melts the animal fat and ocher this young girl used for her hairdo.

THE DIMEKA MARKET

OPPORTUNITIES FOR SOCIAL CONTACTS

A girl goes to market with the merchandise
she will sell or trade.

456

While waiting to sell their wares, these women joke and chatter. In almost all cases their backs are scarred, a result of the flogging rite connected to the Jumping ceremony.

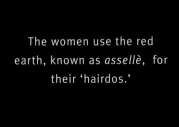

The women use the red
earth, known as *assellè*, for
their 'hairdos.'

A group of girls chews
on roots while chatting
at the Dimeka market.

Braids, colored glass beads and gaudy ear disks lend a singular elegance to this girl.

[GIANNI GIANSANTI]

THE JUMPING CEREMONY

FIVE LEAPS TO BECOME AN ADULT

DURING MY STAY WITH THE HAMER, NOT A DAY PASSED THAT I DIDN'T ASK FOR INFORMATION REGARDING THE JUMPING CEREMONY, THE MOST IMPORTANT INITIATION RITUAL OF THIS ETHNIC GROUP.

And I think that during his lifetime, not a day passed that Sudu did not ask the same questions, waiting anxiously to have a try at the jump. So finally, after having waited for it and pursued it for so long, I was told one afternoon that the event was scheduled for the following day, and that Sudu would face this trial in a place that was yet to be decided upon. Sudu would therefore make the passage from adolescence to adulthood and become a man. And, as the hero for a day, he would have to jump onto bulls in front of all the screaming, merrymaking villagers. The importance of this ritual is rooted in motivations that I know nothing about. What counts is one's capacity to overpower the animals, the agility one displays in doing so. Or does the ritual emphasize the distinction between what a man can do and what a child cannot do? Be that as it may, that day it was essential that Sudu become an adult. Like any self-respecting tradition, this one was accompanied by a series of related celebrations, rituals within the ritual: the dance, the *barra*, the flogging. On that day, from early morning on, there was a holiday atmosphere, the feeling of a great event. The jumping had not yet begun but one could sense it everywhere. The girls walked quickly to gather in the clearing, where the food for the festivities would be prepared.

They all carried a trumpet that they would play for the entire day: the sound of this instrument would accompany even the slightest movement, continuously and incessantly. Another site was the gathering place for the *maz*, the boys who had already brilliantly passed the jumping trial and thus had the right to be the godfathers or sponsors of the next round of jumping rituals. It was they who decided where the ceremony would take place, how many bulls would take part, and how; above all, they would accompany the youth who was to be put to the test. But perhaps that day they had decided to make Sudu wait even longer than usual, because they couldn't come to an agreement as to where the bulls were to be placed: each time they arrived at a level stretch of land that seemed to be suitable for the ceremony, they decided – for reasons unknown to me and that remained unexplained – that this was not the right place. So then the search for the venue began anew. Only around six in the evening did the *maz* find what they were looking for: a plot of flat land on a hill, which would be ideal as the open-air theater where the Hamer villagers could witness Sudu's performance. The women had spent the morning cooking and preparing the food, that is, kneading the sorghum dough with milk in a pumpkin shell bowl, to the sound of the trumpets, with their children always by their side. Once the food had been prepared it was time for the flogging. Contrary to what I had thought, I saw that it was the women, armed with whips

made of rope or reed bushes, who went to the men to provoke them, demanding to be flogged. But the men were taken up with other things: they wanted to enjoy waiting for Sudu, or check on the cattle, or do anything else except whip the women. They truly did not seem at all interested. And paradoxically, flogging them seemed to be an act of grace. Once they were flogged, the women displayed all their masochistic pleasure, despite the fact that their backs were covered with wounds that would leave scars that bore witness to their courage or was proof of the interest that a man had shown in them. Young and beautiful Hamer girls, adolescents and women made their goatskin dresses, glass beads, and decorative shells bob up and down in harmonious dances, leaps and movements, to the sound of singing and trumpets. But the jumping trial was the real reason why the women cooked and played the trumpets, why the

men whipped them, why the *maz* made their decisions, and why the people danced. And the selected youth for the jumping ceremony this time was none other than Sudu. The long-awaited moment arrived at sunset in that clearing that bore little similarity to a theater. Everything was ready: the six bulls had been placed side by side; the girls, on one side, stopped dancing and looked toward the middle of the clearing, smiling and murmuring among themselves; the *maz* moved aside. Sudu leaped, and truth to say, it was not a difficult jump. He jumped without making a mistake, five times. The only thing he had to do to pass the Trial of Life was not to fall. The bulls did not move and he did not fall, so he passed the test. Everything said and done, the fact that the bulls were really cows and that they looked at Sudu tiredly while he celebrated his victory by running off by himself into the forest, was not important. Sudu had become a man.

The men prepare for the festivities by
painting one another's faces and bodies.

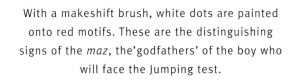
With a makeshift brush, white dots are painted onto red motifs. These are the distinguishing signs of the *maz*, the 'godfathers' of the boy who will face the Jumping test.

The ritual motifs that characterize
the painting decoration are recurrent,
but they highlight a certain creativity
that could be called 'artistic.'

The colors used consist of a mixture
of clay, oils and plant pigments.

474 The Hamer

From 474 to 479 The ritual
flogging begins: women invite
recalcitrant men to flog them
with thin canes.

The backs of these women bear evident marks of the
flogging, the ceremony that, like other rituals, is a
passionate prologue to the Jumping ritual.

The wounds inflicted by the flogging are deep and will leave
permanent scars.

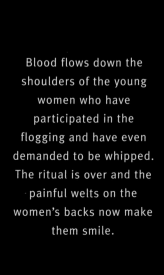

Blood flows down the shoulders of the young women who have participated in the flogging and have even demanded to be whipped. The ritual is over and the painful welts on the women's backs now make them smile.

As is so typical of the spirit of the Hamer, frenzied
dances accompany all festive occasions.

The women are more active in the period preceding the ceremony, which is dedicated to singing and dancing.

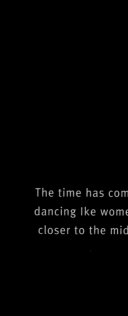

The time has come for the ceremony:
dancing Ike women from nearby draw
closer to the middle of the clearing.

The animals on which the initiate has to
jump are lined up in the chosen site.

According to tradition, bulls should be used for the ceremony, but they are now replaced by cows, which are much easier to find in this poor region.

498-499 and 500-501
The ceremony is over.
The protagonist has passed
the test without making any
mistakes and is now getting
ready for his personal
celebration. The women are
preparing the food that will be
served at the banquet.

BIOGRAPHIES

GIANNI GIANSANTI was born in 1956. Committed to a career as a photojournalist, he began to work for the Sygma Agency in 1981. During the past decades he has photographed and reported on headline news all over the world – including the coup d'état in Turkey and front-page events in El Salvador, Guatemala, Libya, Lebanon, Senegal, Poland, Greece and Yugoslavia and other places. In 1988 he spent three months documenting the private life of John Paul II at the Vatican, a project that won him first prize at the World Press Awards. In 1991 he published the book *Cavalli al Palio*. In 1992 he won the University of Missouri Picture of the Year Award for his work in Somalia during the famine, and also published a text and photographic book on the phenomenon of miracles. In 1993 Giansanti began to work in the world of Formula 1 racing, which resulted in the publication of *The Colors of Passion*, produced with Renault Motorsport. In 1995, publication of *John Paul II: Portrait of a Pope* was followed by prestigious exhibitions of Giansanti's photographs in the Sistine Salon in the Vatican, the Carrousel du Louvre in Paris, and the Museum of Fine Arts in Rio de Janeiro. In 1997 Giansanti published the book *Jacques Villeneuve: A Champion in Pictures*, and in 1999 he told the story of the British-American Racing Team with the books *Realisation of a Dream* and *From Dream to Reality*.

Giansanti is also very interested in art, as is shown by his book *Marcus Aurelius*, produced with the Allianz Insurance Company. This volume is a complete documentation of the restoration work carried out on the famous statue of Marcus Aurelius, one of Rome's greatest emperors. He dedicated the year 1999 to politics, with publication of *Discover the Chamber of Deputies*, focusing on the everyday life backstage at Montecitorio. Throughout 2001 he followed the Italian soccer star Alessandro Del Piero, producing the book *Semplicemente del Piero*. In 2002 he followed the soccer world championships, which resulted in the book *Mondiale in Giallo*, a photographic record of a trip through Korea and Japan during the World Cup.

His most recent work is *A Day on Stage*. Undertaken in collaboration with the Renault Formula I team, it documents the daily events of the French racing team in the factory and at various Grand Prix events.

www.giansanti.com

PAOLO NOVARESIO, born in Turin in 1954, Paolo Novaresio graduated in Contemporary History. He is a traveler, historian and writer who has always been interested in the methodology of exploration. He has made various trips by car, on foot and using local transport in the less visited areas of Africa: from the Sahara to the Congo basin, and in eastern and southern Africa. He has sailed down stretches of the Nile, the Aruwimi and across Lake Tanganyika. He has also explored on foot vast regions of the Sahara and the Suguta valley in Kenya. After a long crossing of the Dark Continent, he spent from 1981 to 1983 in Kenya studying the culture and movements of the Samburu and Turkana nomadic peoples. He has recently concentrated his research in Kenya, Botswana, Namibia and South Africa. He also works on the logistical preparations for scientific expeditions and explorations, and writes on African history and civilizations for various magazines and newspapers. For Edizioni White Star he wrote the text for *Men Toward the Unknown* (1997).

BIBLIOGRAPHY

Isack H. A., *Boran* (Nairobi: Evans Brothers, 1986)

Amin, M., *Cradle of Mankind* (New York: The Overlook Press, 1983)

Beckwitt, C. and Fisher, A., *African Ark: People and Ancient Cultures of Ethiopia and the Horn of Africa* (New York: Harry Abrams, 1990)

Brown, M., *Where Giants Trod* (London: Quiller Press, 1989)

Castiglioni, Angelo and Alfredo, *Venere Nera* (Varese: Edizioni Lativa, 1985)

Castiglioni Angelo and Alfredo, and Salvioni, G., *Lo specchio scuro di Adamo* (Varese: Edizioni Lativa, 1987)

Cerulli, E., *Peoples of South-West Ethiopia and Its Borderland*, (London: International African Institute, 1956)

Encyclopedia Aethiopica – Vol. I. (Wiesbaden: Harrassowitz, 2003)

Hayward, D., *The Arbore Language: a First Investigation* (Hamburg: Helmut Buske Verlag, 1984)

von Honel, L., *Discovery by Count Teleki of Lake Rudolf and Stefanie* (London: Frank Cass & Co., 1968, reprint)

Smith, A. Donaldson, *Through Unknown African Countries* (New York: Greenwood Publishers, 1969 reprint)

Strecker, I. and Lydall, J.R., *The Hamar of Southern Ethiopia: 1. Work Journal; 2. Baldambe Explains; 3. Conversations in Dambaiti* (Hohenschaftlarn: Klaus Renner, 1979)

Semplici, A., *Etiopia* (Milan: ClupGuide, UTET Libreria, 1996)

Tadesse, W.G., *Property and Age Organisation among an East African Pastoralist Group* (Max Plank Institute for Social Anthropology, Working Paper no. 14, 2000)

Tosco, M., *The Dhaasanac Language* (Cologne: Rudiger Koppe Verlag, 2001)

Vannutelli, L. and Citerni, C., *L' Omo* (Milan: Hoepli Editore, 1899)

THE AUTHOR AND THE PUBLISHER WOULD LIKE TO THANK:

Ethiopian Airlines
KEL 12
Paolo Ruffa

H.E. Ambassador Guido Latella,
Dr. Emiliano Longhi, Director of Istituto di Cultura of the Italian Embassy in Ethiopia,
and also H.E. Ambassador Mengistu Hulluka,
Consul Mekkonen Gossaye and Fortuna Dibaco of the Ethiopian Embassy in Italy for generous and
valuable assistance with this book.

Thanks are also due to:

Riccardo Auci, Claudio Bassi, Zinabu Berhe, Aldo Bonzi, Giovanna Calvenzi, Jean François Caubet, Nancy Dahl Paradisi
Dompè, Ernesto De Vizio, Alessandro di Napoli, Massimo Di Rienzo, Stefano Folgaria, Andrea Giansanti, Solomon Gizaw,
Daniele Guglielmi, Maria Mann, Luca Mazzocco, Maurizio Melloni, Arnaldo Minuti, Carlotta Perazzi, Riccardo Scoma, Paolo
Secondino, Assunta Servello, Gabriella Squillace, Patrizia Spinelli, Brian Storm, Enrico Tedeschi, Yohannes Teshale, Luigi
Toma, Ala Tozzi, Guillaume Valabregue, Carlo Verdelli, Susan Welchman, Michael Yamashita, Anaylem, Romeo.